# Ocean of Storms, Sea of Disaster

## North Atlantic Shipwrecks of the Strange and Curious

### Robert C. Parsons

Pottersfield Press, Lawrencetown Beach, Nova Scotia, Canada

**Library and Archives Canada Cataloguing in Publication**

Parsons, Robert Charles, 1944-

Ocean of storms, sea of disaster : North Atlantic shipwrecks of the strange and curious / Robert C. Parsons.

ISBN 1-895900-74-3

1. Shipwrecks--North Atlantic Ocean.  2. Curiosities and wonders--North Atlantic Ocean. I. Title.

G525.P372 2005          910'.9163'4      C2005-902636-7

Cover design: Dalhousie Design Services

Pottersfield Press acknowledges the ongoing support of The Canada Council for the Arts, and the financial support of the Government of Canada through the Book Publishing Industry Development Program for our publishing activities. We also acknowledge the support of the Nova Scotia Department of Tourism, Culture and Heritage.

Pottersfield Press
83 Leslie Road
East Lawrencetown
Nova Scotia, Canada, B2Z 1P8
Website: www.pottersfieldpress.com
To order, phone 1-800-NIMBUS9 (1-800-646-2879)
Printed in Canada

 Canada Council    Conseil des Arts        Canadä         NOVA SCOTIA
for the Arts      du Canada                              Tourism, Culture and Heritage

# Contents

# Foreword

Over the past one hundred and fifty years countless shipwrecks have occurred in the North Atlantic. Many have been forgotten; others became well-known for a variety of reasons. Some are remembered because of the large number of lives lost, others for the social importance of the victims at the time of the disaster. Still others are famous because of their valuable cargoes or the ship was and still is of historical significance. A few ships are well-known because they are spectacular or accessible dive sites.

This collection of tales of shipwrecks delves not so much into the well-known as into the strange, curious, odd marine disasters. The locale is mainly the northwestern Atlantic Ocean. Many of the ships presented are more obscure, but equally fascinating. *Ocean of Storms, Sea of Disaster* does not re-examine the "famous" and the minutely analyzed ship losses of the Atlantic. Nor will you find "inland" stories – for example, the wreck of the *Edmund Fitzgerald* or the great disaster that befell the *General Slocum* in New York's East River. Shipping losses due to enemy action in World Wars I and II are few in this book, choosing as I did some rare or strange ship loss. Most tales of the war eras resulted from ships which encountered all-powerful and ever-present forces of wind, wave, fog and rock.

Arbitrarily, I chose a time range of one hundred years, between 1846 and 1947. By the mid-point of the twentieth century the great wind-driven schooners had all but disappeared; intercontinental airplanes and jumbo jets hastened the demise of passenger liners and large cargo-carrying steamers. By then, too, great improvements in communication, navigational aids and long range weather forecasting substantially reduced ship losses.

This research and the writing of *Ocean of Storms, Sea of Disaster* began about 1995 when I searched for information and details of eastern Canada's (the Atlantic Provinces) ship losses and wrecks. In the course of reading through Nova Scotia, Newfoundland, New Brunswick and Prince Edward Island newspapers, I inadvertently found obscure or strange stories of steamers, freighters, ocean liners and schooners from other lands. These tales looked good to me and I thought they would be interesting to anyone who wanted a mysterious or unique sea yarn or two. In time, I arranged, collated, further researched, and wrote the stories.

In the spring of 2005, my publisher and mentor at Pottersfield Press, Lesley Choyce, liked the idea of North Atlantic shipwrecks and wanted "to take a look at the manuscript." Because of his faith in me and because he published my first Nova Scotian work – *In Peril on the Sea: Shipwrecks of Nova Scotia* – several years ago (plus he had some very encouraging words to say of my research/writing), I wish to dedicate this collection to Lesley of Pottersfield Press.

Robert C. Parsons
32 Pearson Place
Grand Bank, Newfoundland, A0E 1W0
E-mail: robertparsons@personainternet.com
Website: http://shipwrecks.nf.ca

# 1

## Wrecks: Legacy of the Atlantic

*March 1846*

One of the most fascinating and thought-provoking things you can look at is a wreck chart of the North Atlantic coast. Yet it brings a sense of pathos and wonder at the senseless waste, the squander of lives, ships, cargoes. The losses of ships and lives had devastating financial and personal effects on families, communities and local economies.

According to the *New York Herald's* reckoning (in a November 1893 account), nearly a thousand ships had been dashed to pieces within five years from 1888 to 1893 on the North Atlantic coast alone, and even the graves of these ships "trace out a curious curve of a thousand other hulks drifting about on the wild waste of waters." And that five-year span can be multiplied over and over in the era of high traffic on North Atlantic shipping lanes.

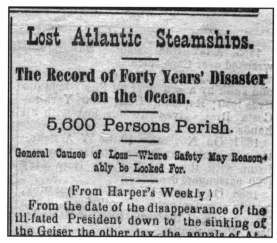

**Lost Atlantic Steamships.**

**The Record of Forty Years' Disaster on the Ocean.**

**5,600 Persons Perish.**

General Causes of Loss—Where Safety May Reasonably be Looked For.

(From Harper's Weekly)
From the date of the disappearance of the ill-fated President down to the sinking of the Geiser the other day, the annals of At...

The St. John's, Newfoundland, *Evening Mercury* of October 16, 1888, carried the *Harper's Weekly* list of forty years of steamship losses. These were losses from the great steamers, yet there were many more people who perished in smaller, less-heralded ships.

In the period of all-sail wooden ships and the passenger-cargo steamers, an average of more than two thousand vessels and twelve thousand lives were lost in the various seas every year. The value of ships and cargoes was estimated to be $100 million annually. Many of these went down in the North Atlantic – not only one of the most stormy and treacherous oceans of the world, but also one which saw a tremendous volume of traffic between Europe and the New World.

Many of these ships were lost in strange and curious circumstances, ranging from piracy, fire, mutiny, disappearances and unexplained explosions. Collisions were frequent: with other ships, icebergs, whales, logs, derelicts. Some were struck by lightning, shelled by enemy submarines, or crushed by ice. There were times when new, seaworthy and strong ships were swallowed up by a seemingly innocent windstorm they should have weathered. Others, apparently frail, leaky ships, came through violent hurricanes and gales unharmed. The sea was then – as it is now – unfathomable, mysterious, treacherous.

Up to 1893, the newspapers of the day believed that no one had investigated with "sufficient accuracy" all the relative losses of lives and ships from Newfoundland to the West Indies – the shores of these places were strewn with wrecks and graves. With such a proliferation of shipwrecks, it is only possible in this volume to skim some of the more strange, fascinating and tragic calamities in the earlier years. Of some marine disasters, little has been documented.

But even that "little" can be thought-provoking: often major disasters were reported in just a few words in news media of the day. Investigations, marine courts of inquiry and probes searching for the cause of shipwreck, collision, or disappearance were the exception rather than the rule.


In March 1846, the line packet ship *Henry Clay* flew before a terrific gale. It struck the shore at Squan Beach, New Jersey, at midnight. There it lay, thumping on the sand, while its frenzied crew and passengers threw two hundred bags of salt overboard. The crew cut away masts to ease the strain on the stranded hull.

Two hundred and seventy passengers sailed on *Henry Clay* and for the most part they all kept their courage. In the early morning light of the new day, they saw a crowd of men on the beach, preparing to save them. The second mate and four men succeeded in getting a line ashore. When darkness came on again a crew of fearless surfmen from the nearby lifesaving station managed to reach the wreck, but Captain Nye of *Henry Clay* would not attempt to land the passengers in such a sea.

## THE RECENT STORMS:
### WRECK OF A BARQUE AT BALITHAM, NEAR PLYMOUTH

If rescuers could get a breeches buoy or a rope aboard a ship, it was not always successful, as this image from the *Illustrated London News* of November 13, 1880, shows. Often the connection broke or slack rope dropped and dipped weary seamen into the seas. Or, as is the case here, when a breeches buoy reached the wreck of a barque near Plymouth, England, exhausted sailors were too weak to hold on.

All night the storm increased and the passengers were overcome with terror. Strong men, who previously thought themselves fearless, went into fits of despair and the women and children lay about in groups dumb with fear.

At dawn, the Jerseymen were ready. The ship had worked around with its stern toward the beach. Nye rigged a derrick or breeches buoy on the taffrail (the rail around the vessel's stern) to which a strong hawser was secured. The other end was hauled to the shore and made fast.

At first the ship's crew tried a hogshead of salt. It went to the shore by means of a traveler line (to carry the weight) and a hauler line. Then in twos and threes the passengers and crew crawled into the empty barrel and were hauled across the booming, white-jawed breakers without even getting their feet wet.

The New Jersey surfmen, however, worked for hours up to their necks in water; in the end all but six of the ship's complement were rescued.

# 2

## Fire on the Amazon

*January 1852*

In the first eleven years of its existence, England's West India Steam Packet Company lost eight of its fleet. The *Medina* hit a coral reef near Turks Island; the *Isis* sunk off Bermuda; the *Solway* wrecked off Spain; the *Tweed* and the *Forth* foundered on Alacranes Rocks in the Gulf of Mexico; the *Actolon* was lost in the Mediterranean; and the newest steamer *Demerara* was stranded in the River Avon, England, in 1852, shortly before the company's most devastating loss, the *Amazon*.

Built in Green's shipyards at Blackwall in the fall of 1851, the paddlewheel steamer *Amazon* was new, right off the stocks, and had only been on one short trial run. Its first paying voyage would be from England to the West Indies and Gulf of Mexico with mail and passengers. To ensure its success and that nothing could go wrong, the company put Captain Symonds, one of the best in the business, in command.

*Amazon*, with 161 crew and passengers, mail and a valuable cargo – part of which was five thousand bottles of quicksilver worth more than £5,000 – left Liverpool on January 2, 1852. On January 6, while well out in the Atlantic, the ship caught fire.

At midnight, the officer on watch had occasion to go as far as the fore hold and saw flames licking up from the galley. He gave the alarm to Captain Symonds and they set the fire alarm bell ringing. Immediately, passengers and crew aroused from sleep came scrambling up on deck, many nearly naked. The flames soon burst out from the engine room and ignited the hay for livestock.

The flames spread from end to end of the ship with lightning speed. *Amazon's* officers ordered out the boats, woefully inadequate for twenty crew and about 140 passengers. A subsequent report says: "The captain ordered the ship to be put before the wind and the engines to be stopped, but so great a hold had the fire obtained that the engineers and firemen were unable to remain below. They could not get at the engines to stop them.

"At this time, less than half an hour from the discovery of the fire and when it had obtained such a mastery as to baffle the exertions of officers and crew, the flames ascended and cut off all communication. The vessel was still under steam.

"Efforts were made to launch the best lifeboat, but the flames prevented the crew from getting to it. They went to the second boat, just abaft the sponson [a triangular platform near the paddlebox] on the port side."

The seas that night were high. To get any boats over the side in the dark while the ship was steaming ahead must have been a daunting, or nigh impossible, task for even the most seasoned seamen. The crew lowered the mail boat on the port side with about twenty people in it. That boat swamped alongside and all aboard perished. The pinnace was lowered, but the seas swept all hands out of it.

On the starboard side, seamen and passengers steadily lowered the gig, full of people. The second cutter in front of the gig was lowered down, but a sea struck its bow and unhooked the tackle. As the *Amazon* rose in the seas, it lifted the cutter by the stern tackle and tipped all but two people out into the sea. These two hung on, doubled over the boat's thwarts, screaming for help.

Number Two lifeboat, also on the starboard side, was lowered and drifted clear of the burning *Amazon*, but flew through the seas, driven by wind and wave, at a fearful pace. The only boat lowered without mishap was the little dingy. This carried five people in the charge of crewman Mr. Vincent, but was so low in the water it would surely swamp. Those in the dingy reached the Number Two lifeboat and were taken aboard.

The first work of those aboard the lifeboat was to stabilize the boat and to get back to the doomed ship to assist if possible. Attempts to reach the burning ship were defeated by high seas, which tore off the lifeboat's rudder and nearly filled the craft with water. There was nothing to do except to bring its head into the wind, to watch the seas, and to pull at the oars to meet the waves head on.

While in this unenviable position, those in the lifeboat could see the *Amazon* in the distance right ahead, burning from stem to stern. The blaze lit up the sky and sea for miles around. They could see the funnels glow red-hot and, as the lifeboat drifted past the stern about a half mile away, the magazine exploded, discharging a number of rocket flares. It was 5:30 a.m.

About half an hour after the funnels went over the side, *Amazon* sank beneath the waves. Pitch blackness replaced the red illumination from the ship. Long before *Amazon* disap-

Shipboard fire is a treacherous enemy, as this December 5, 1865, image from the *Illustrated London News* demonstrates. To wait too long to launch a lifeboat could be disastrous. Wind from the moving vessel would fan the flames, preventing the crew from getting the boats over the side. To stay aboard was to face death by fire. In the illustration, the blaze has a firm hold on dry wood, sails and ropes on a windjammer, just as it did on the steam/paddle ship *Amazon* in 1852.

peared for good, everyone left on board must have either drowned or been burned to death.

According to the report, "A gentleman and a lady in their night dresses only, both on fire, came on deck, and with their arms around each other, walked over to one of the ship's hatches and fell together into the flames."

At noon the next day, those in the lifeboat, in Mr. Neilson's charge, were still adrift without rudder, compass, water, or food, but with oars. They saw a brig heading in their direction. It was the *Marsden*, sailing from London to South Carolina. Captain Evans and his crew gave the boat's crew from *Amazon* a berth to sleep in, food and sympathy. *Marsden* scoured the area where the ship went down and kept a lookout on the masthead. There was nothing to be seen.

A group in the mail boat, which had successfully gotten away after having been swamped, were picked up by a Dutch vessel and landed at Brest, France. Neither the gig nor those aboard were ever seen again. In total, eighteen members of the crew, two women and an eighteen-month-old baby were rescued from *Amazon*.

One of the firemen who survived claimed the fire originated from the overheating of the cranks and other parts of the steam and paddle machinery. It was necessary to cool it down with water frequently. The heat from this and from the steam boilers must have ignited the wood casing around the steam chest.

# 3

## William and Mary:
## A captain's cover-up?

Safe and sound in the lifeboat, Captain Stinson, his mates and some sailors left the sinking *William and Mary*. There were not enough lifeboats for all, so the officers of the ship took the best available and abandoned those left aboard to their fate – a certain death, so they thought.

On May 17, 1853, the *New York Daily Times* in its brief article on the wreck of *William and Mary* said: "A vessel arrived in New York, bringing the captain, mate and six crew from Liverpool to New Orleans with railway iron. It struck Bermuda, May 3, and nearly all of 282 passengers went down. Only a few passengers saved."

By the next day the *New York Daily Times* had inter-viewed Captain Stinson and one of the sailors and ran a longer version of the great disaster of the *William and Mary*: "At 4 a.m. May 4th, said Stinson, the weather became squally with a heavy sea and there was eight feet of water in the hold. [At this time many passengers, including Joseph Brooke, were below deck, asleep, or unaware of the actions of the crew.]

"The ship was beginning to sink – the leak was gaining rapidly. The greatest terror now prevailed. The passengers made frantic attempts to free the boats and launch them. They crowded about the gangways and raised a deafening clamor.

"In the confusion, two boats were stove in and made use-less. The lifeboat and longboat were gotten out safely and to their preservation is due the rescue of the few remaining per-sons of the crew and passengers.

"The emigrants, unskilled in the management of the boats, precipitated their own fate. The boats were crowded with men, women and children, while yet hanging from the davits. At 8 a.m. the vessel was abandoned by her officers and she went down a few minutes afterward.

"Upon the deck was left the entire number of passengers on board, with the exception of the thirty or so in the long-boat. The screams and appeals for aid from the decks of the ill-fated ship still linger upon the ears of the few survivors."

The daily newspaper also developed its story of the wreck from the tale of a Danish seaman who had been rescued from the lifeboat. His story seemed to confirm the captain's. Such yells "of the unfortunate wretches who were left to perish were unearthly" and each in the vernacular of Irish, Dutch, German. They implored for help from quarters where there was none – no people, no objects. There was not a loose spar, mast or hatch cover and the last two lifeboats were damaged.

The Danish sailor estimated that when the vessel went down, those left on board numbered no less than 170 and could have been as high as 185. Those surviving were Captain Stinson, his mates, six sailors and about thirty passengers – one group picked up by the ship *Reuben Carter*, the other by an English schooner.

Many questions, said the daily paper, remained unanswered: Had the *William and Mary* been driven upon a reef that was well-known and clearly marked on all charts? Why had the captain secured only a handful of worthless papers and left behind his log, journal and other important documents? Most importantly, why did so many of the crew get in lifeboats and why were nearly all the passengers left to drown like rats on a sinking ship? Why had the captain and crew of the *William and Mary* left the Bahamas and the Indies to come north to New York so quickly?

In addition, no one seemed to know the names of those lost in the supposed "catastrophe." In conclusion, the newspaper said: "A terrible loss of life is undoubtedly the result of this calamity, and the long catalogue of disasters receives a melancholy addition. Further developments, by the action of the owners and the Captain, will be awaited with great interest."

However, one expression of interest came from passenger Joseph Brooke, no doubt determined to set the record straight. He helped bring the strange actions of *William and Mary*'s officers to their just and final conclusion. Brooke had seen the captain's report of the voyage. He had heard and read other various tales and believed some accounts of the disaster were not only misleading, but were downright lies or had vital parts left out. To set the record straight Brooke published his own account, printed first in the *New Orleans Picayune* and then in the *New York Daily Times* of July 4, 1853.

Most passengers on the *William and Mary*, Brooke said, were from Germany, Holland and the north of Ireland. Things went well for nearly the whole voyage, but on May 2, that changed. Captain Stinson expected to make the Bahamas before daylight and sent three crewmen forward as lookouts.

About 12:30 a.m. the captain said to the mate he was sure land was near, as he could tell by the sound of the water and waves. The mate ran forward and sure enough they were nearly upon the land. The helm was put hard to port, but the rocks were not more than one mile ahead. *William and Mary* at the time was skimming along at seven knots an hour.

A man was sent aloft to see if he could see the Hole in the Wall Light, which was sighted about three hours later. At 12 o'clock on May 3, the ship passed the Stirrup Key. Captain Stinson then spoke to a group of passengers. Passenger Brooke recalled: "About 8 o'clock in the evening the captain came on deck and told me he should not go to bed that night, as he was in a very dangerous place. He showed the position of the ship by tracing in a rough manner her course with a penknife on the deck. He said that near about was a sunken rock and he did not know exactly where it was. From that time he began to get visibly agitated. I spoke to him, but could get no answer."

About 8:30 the ship struck, very gently and stayed so still Brooke thought it drifted off the ledge. The sailors mustered around, raising or lowering sails. Captain Stinson asked the mate if the ship went ahead at all. "Not a damn bit!" he said.

The next order was to get out the boats with the passengers helping. One was lowered safely, four sailors climbed in and, as a precaution, tied the craft to the *William and Mary* and remained there all night.

Meanwhile, according to passenger Brooke, the jolly boat was hanging at the davits in the aft part of the ship. Many passengers crowded into this and although they were told the weight would break the boat, some refused to leave it. Consequently, the stern rope of the boat gave away and it hung solely by the bow rope with the stern of the jolly boat in the water. Fortunately no lives were lost in this mishap. Crew and passengers lowered another boat. Orders came to let it go astern, but this boat struck the one dangling by one rope and both were stove in and useless.

Brooke recalled: "About three hours after we struck, the captain called all the male passengers together, and told them that he expected that as the tide rose the ship would float off the rock. If all hands would try to keep the vessel afloat by working the pumps until morning, he would be able to run the ship to ashore. Everything would be saved. Accordingly we went to the pumps and worked as men whose lives depended on their exertions. We had not been long at the pumps before the ship went off the rock. Immediately the anchor was let go."

By 2 a.m. on May 4, the passengers had been at the pumps about three hours. The mate came to them, saying everything was alright. There was only three feet of water in the hold, he said, and the pumpers were reducing that.

It seemed as if the stranded ship would not go to pieces. All felt more at ease. But Joseph Brooke was in for a surprise. He was still worried and went up on deck at daylight only to find the first and second mate sitting in the lifeboat attached to the side of *William and Mary*. The other sailors had been working on another boat, the longboat, getting it shipshape and ready for launching. Immediately, he was suspicious. Brooke went to the captain and accused him of intending to desert the ship and leave the passengers behind to fend for themselves.

"Sir, you and your crew are deserting this ship."

"I intend no such thing," he said. "As long as you and the other passengers man the pumps I'll not leave this ship."

Yet within the next few hours Captain Stinson slipped into the lifeboat with the mates and some of the sailors and rowed away, thus deserting *William and Mary*. As Brooke said after, "They left us all to perish."

By 7 a.m. utter confusion erupted. When the longboat was lowered, the passengers made a simultaneous and mad rush to get into it. Twenty-five – far too many – jumped in, with three more in the water holding on to a rope still attached to the longboat. One of the sailors cut the rope with a hatchet and these three went under water and perished.

"Now commenced a scene," said Brooke, "that is almost impossible to describe. When this last boat was cut adrift, it was found some men in it had left their wives behind on the ship, some had left fathers and mothers, others left brothers and sisters."

The people thus left on a sinking ship with no lifeboat and no obvious way of surviving began crying, screaming, and tearing their hair. They would call to those in the boat, saying, "Come back, let us all die together."

One woman, whose husband was in the lifeboat, was so enraged by his cowardly conduct, she took off her wedding ring and threw it at her husband, muttering something in German (which Brooke admitted he didn't understand, but her actions spoke louder than words).

"We were now," said Brooke, "in a most painful condition – no boat, with no one who knew where we were, or who could tell us what to do. We agreed after council together, to slip the cable and try to make the land which we had passed the previous day.

"The first thing though was to get the pumps going again; they having been stopped while the longboat was being lowered. We slipped the cable and away we drifted. We now tried to get the sails up, but during the night the braces fore and aft had been cut. We were at the mercy of the waves and had no idea where we were going.

"At 12 o'clock it was proposed we make some rafts, hoping to save some people by that means if the ship went down before assistance came. We constructed two rafts, capable of holding fifty people each. At five in the afternoon we saw a ship, but it didn't see us.

"Darkness was gathering fast. Not one of us still aboard thought we would ever see the morning. We had a dreadful storm during the night – rain in torrents, accompanied by thunder and lightning. We were getting fatigued as we worked hard at the pumps. However, in the midst of our troubles daylight broke and we saw land ahead about eight miles away. Soon after, we saw a vessel making toward us.

"By 9:30 she came alongside and proved to be the *Oracle*, Captain Sands of Elbow Key. He immediately agreed to take the women on his ship, land them and to come back to try to get our ship ashore."

By the next day, it was determined the *William and Mary* could not be salvaged and Captain Sands, with another vessel, the *Contest*, rescued the remaining people. The erstwhile brig went down about thirty miles from the Bahamas.

Brooke concludes his report, saying, "Vessels were found to take us to our destination and we left for New Orleans on June 1, making a total of seventy-seven days since we left Liverpool."

# 4

## The curious cause of Humboldt's wreck

*December 1853*

"Without a moment's delay, two discharges of cannon announce the departure of the *Humboldt*. Every officer, pilot and sailor is at his post. The captain with his speaking trumpet orders the departure and the steamer steers her course for the coasts of England where English passengers and mails are received."

Thus did "a man of the cloth," a Roman Catholic Jesuit missionary, describe leaving Europe in November 1853. Brother Pierre Jean DeSmet left Ghent, Belgium, travelled to Le Havre, France, and then sailed for New York. There were twelve young brothers with him as well many other passengers on the steamer *Humboldt*. Passengers were of every faith and creed and, as DeSmet discovered, were not shy about expressing their opinions.

But his voyage, which began cheerfully, ended with fear and a new appreciation for the dangers of sea voyages. Fortunately for posterity, many priests and brothers kept detailed journals of their lives and travels; thus DeSmet's description of hardship at sea and shipwreck was sent back to Brussels.

By December 3, the *Humboldt* was out into the tossing, angry Atlantic. It had fought a stormy sea and a violent west wind. "Neptune," writes DeSmet, "received a fitting tribute from those who were so bold as to hazard crossing his domain in this season of the year."

Several clergy were confined to bed constantly. Seasickness was the order of the day. But to add to those human shortcomings, Brother DeSmet told of other disagreeable circumstances: "The steam engine got out of order several times and the boilers threatened to blow us into the air. The coal was of bad quality and even that became scarce on the twelfth day of our voyage. We were obliged to get a supply of coal at Halifax, a seaport of Nova Scotia. This neglect on the part of the company, the owners of *Humboldt*, was extremely fatal in its consequences."

On December 6, about fifteen miles from Halifax a fisherman presented himself on board as a pilot and declared to the captain, who demanded his certificates or qualifications as a harbour pilot, "that his papers were either in his boat, or at his own house."

*Humboldt*'s captain relied on his word and entrusted a stranger, perhaps unqualified in pilotage, to bring the steamer past the rocky hazards off Halifax. Against the express opinion of the officers, the spurious pilot changed the ship's direction. An argument broke out, but the pilot persisted in his stubbornness.

De Smet describes in his diary what happened next: "An hour and a half afterwards, the *Humboldt* struck on the dangerous rocks called The Sisters in the neighbourhood of Devil's Island [at the mouth of Halifax harbour]. It was half-past six in the morning. The greater number of the passengers were still in their berths. The shock was terrific. I was walking on the deck at the moment. Discovering directly great pieces of wood floating on the surface of the water, I hastened to warn all my companions of their danger for they were still in their beds.

"Young Hegel had been entrusted to me by his father and I took him by my side as long as danger lasted. I kept a rope in my hand for the purpose of lowering him into the first lifeboat that should be launched.

"Fear had palsied every heart and while the water was pouring in the *Humboldt* by torrents, fire broke out. It was gotten under control by great exertion and through the presence of mind of the first engineer. After great efforts, the crew succeeded in extinguishing it.

"As if all things conspired to our destruction, a fog arose, so thick we could not see thirty paces from the vessel. The whole power of the steam engine was exerted in an attempt to gain the shore six miles distant.

"The ship soon leaned out to the larboard side where it had begun to leak and the ship began to go down. Every arm set to work to aid the launching of the small boats. Had not the captain exhibited great presence of mind and an extraordinary firmness, there would have been much tumult and disorder. There was a rush to get in first, but happily we were not obliged to use the lifeboats to save ourselves.

"While a great number believed that all was lost, and I among the rest, the *Humboldt* touched again, in a few fathoms of water and rested on a rock. We are saved!"

## THE PENINSULAR AND ORIENTAL SCREW-STEAMER JEDDO ASHORE NEAR BOMBAY

In this drawing from the *Illustrated London News*, March 17, 1866, the steamer *Jeddo* is ashore near Bombay (now Mumbai), India. In a similar situation the crew and passengers of the *Humboldt* nearly perished near Halifax, Nova Scotia, in 1853.

The group of clerics, other passengers and crew still had to get off the sinking steamer. DeSmet says, to their joyful surprise, they found the shore was only one hundred feet away. The sea was calm, the wind dropped and the sun came out.

Although all passengers had the good fortune and time to save their trunks and traveling bags, the loss of *Humboldt* and its cargo was estimated at $600,000. The writer made no mention of what retribution came upon "the false pilot" who had led the steamer *Humboldt* to destruction upon Halifax's Sisters Shoals.

DeSmet concludes with a description of his fellow travelers and perhaps another "reason" for the shipwreck: "We had for traveling companions on the *Humboldt*, Jews, Infidels, and Protestants of every shade. Some of the voyagers were imbued with very strong prejudices against the Catholic faith, but in particular against Jesuits. The wreck of the *Humboldt* was even attributed to our presence.

"A few hours after the wreck, a steamboat from Halifax, a place then with a population of about 25,000 souls, came to our aid. The Archbishop of the city treated us with great kindness."

Pierre Jean DeSmet continued to make frequent voyages across the Atlantic in search of missionaries and funds to operate the Catholic missions he had established in the midwest and northwest United States. Born in 1801, the pioneering Jesuit missionary arrived in the United States in 1821. He often served as a peackmaker and mediator between the Northwest and Plains Indian tribes and the United States government, and his books and correspondence are viewed as important sources of Western U.S. history and Indian life. The town of DeSmet, South Dakota, is named after the Belgian missionary, and was also home to Laura Ingalls Wilder, author of *The Little House on the Prairie* books.

# 5

## Wreck of the Arctic

*September 1854*

By the 1850s, England's fleet of transoceanic liners had captured most of the passenger and freight trade in the North Atlantic. Their passenger liners were generally large, fast and luxurious. However, an American shipping magnate, Edward Collins, wanted to cut into the British monopoly.

Collins began working in the business at age fifteen in New York City and bought his first line in 1831. Five years later, he launched the Dramatic Line, a transatlantic carrier whose ships were named after actors. He garnered a Congressional subsidy in 1847 and formed the United States Mail Steamship Company to compete with Britain's Cunard Line. Collins began with four ships – *Atlantic, Pacific, Arctic* and *Baltic* – all named after bodies of water.

If it were not for two tragic events during the 1850s, the Collins Line might have continued its transatlantic service for a much longer time.

In September 1854, his S.S. *Arctic*, a deluxe, wooden-hulled paddle steamer, was bound from New York to England with 135 crewmen and 246 passengers, including the wife and two children of founder Edward Collins. While steaming at high speed off Cape Race, Newfoundland, *Arctic* collided with a French steamer, the iron-hulled *Vesta*. *Vesta* was much smaller and, at first, *Arctic*'s master, Captain James Luce, was convinced the smaller vessel had sustained the greater damage. He was mistaken.

Bound from St. Pierre to Granville, France, the merchant screw steamer *Vesta* had 147 seasonal fishermen aboard and a crew of fifty. *Vesta* was doing about eight knots and, in the impact, its bow was completely shattered and the foremast broken off. One man was killed and others were seriously injured.

It looked like *Vesta* would be the first to sink and many aboard believed the best chance for safety was the *Arctic*. Those on *Vesta* could barely see the other ship through the fog. Some men jumped overboard to get on board *Arctic*, but soon their cries of distress rang out over the water. *Arctic* was slowly drifting away. One of *Vesta*'s lifeboats got away with about fifteen people.

Meanwhile, aboard *Arctic* Captain Luce realized his ship was sinking fast. There was a mad scramble for lifeboats. Utter confusion broke out among the passengers and crew, but a few saner heads manned the pumps and succeeded in lightening the ship forward. They hoped to get at the bow where the worst leaks seemed to be. Many passengers climbed into the lifeboats, which were still hanging in their davits. Forty-five minutes after the collision, Second Officer Baalham went to the captain to report water was up to the lower deck beams and there was no hope of saving the ship. "Go to your lifeboat station," Captain Luce told Baalham, "and lower the boats."

But many of the lifeboats were completely filled with terrified men and women and there was no possibility of getting near them. Three lowered lifeboats disappeared and their whereabouts are still unknown. When *Arctic* went down many people milling about on deck were swept away by seas; others perished sitting in lifeboats, still not lowered.

At 4:45 p.m. *Arctic* gave its final nod and sank. The captain's son was killed when the paddlewheel housing fell off the ship; Luce and a few other survivors crawled atop this structure and they were eventually picked up. The bodies of Collins' wife, son and daughter were not found.

Two lifeboats got away safely and Baalham took charge of both boats. He figured he was less than sixty miles south-southeast of Cape Race. After pulling for forty-two hours with nothing but the run of the sea to guide them, the survivors reached Broad Cove, about twelve miles north of Cape Race. The forty-five survivors left to walk to Renews – a coastal trail, rugged but well-marked. The group reached Renews on Friday, September 29.

Seventy-two men and four women left *Arctic* on a make-shift raft, but only one person aboard it was alive when found two days later.

Meanwhile officers aboard *Vesta* found that its watertight bulkhead had not split or opened, and Captain Duschene saw this as an opportunity to save his ship. He gave orders to lighten his vessel by the bow – fish, cargo and luggage were tossed over the side. This raised the head of the ship considerably and that, coupled with the strength of the forward bulkhead, stopped the heavy inrush of water. The passengers and crew stacked about 150 mattresses and blankets behind the safety partition, over which they threw spare sails. The whole batting was firmly secured by board and planks, tied with cables.

A lithograph by Nathaniel Currier (1813-1888) shows the luxury liner *Arctic* sinking after a collision with *Vesta* off Cape Race in 1854. (From the collection of Captain Hubert Hall, Shipsearch Marine, Yarmouth, Nova Scotia)

The foremast, which had broken off, was cut away and this too helped raise the head of the vessel. This whole operation, done under stress and fear of sinking, took two days. *Vesta* then ran under little steam to St. John's; fortunately, before the rising of a severe gale which came up the evening they sailed in through The Narrows on September 30.

In all, ninety people survived the loss of *Arctic* and nearly three hundred perished. Yet the fate of *Vesta*, which remained afloat through luck, hard work and ingenuity, was nearly forgotten in the annals of dramatic shipwrecks.

Eighteen months later another Collins liner, the *Pacific*, disappeared without a trace. On January 23, 1856, it sailed from Liverpool with eighty passengers. Despite exhaustive searches, no trace of *Pacific* was ever found; it was generally assumed the vessel foundered in mid-Atlantic or struck ice and went down.

EARTHQUAKE WAVE AT ST. THOMAS STRIKING R.M.S. LA PLATA

The *Illustrated London News*, December 28, 1867, shows a paddlewheel steamer like the *Arctic*. Three of *Arctic's* lifeboats were lowered and filled, but they and their passengers were never seen again.

Then in 1986 a fisherman's nets became entangled in the wreck lying in the Irish Sea about twelve miles northeast of Anglesey. This was marked on a chart and in the early 1990s, divers explored the area. They discovered the remains of a ship tentatively identified as *Pacific*, although further investigation may reveal why it sank.

With those two North Atlantic tragedies, the travelling public lost faith in the Collins Line and the shipping company soon faded into obscurity.

# 6

## Bad luck and tragedy stalks New Era

On November 14, 1854, the cholera-ridden ship *New Era* was driven ashore on a sand bar near Corlies Creek on the New Jersey coast. At dawn the great vessel swung around and seas swept over it, tearing away everything on its decks and pounding it furiously against the beach. Aboard were 426 people.

The *New Era* was an emigrant ship of 1,328 tons launched in Bath, Maine, in 1854 and it was on its first voyage. It sailed on September 28 and had been nearly two months on the way. The cargo consisted of five hundred tons of chalk, dry goods and hardware. Nearly all aboard were German passengers, but forty were lost to cholera during the trip.

When *New Era* struck, passengers and crew swarmed up on deck, filling the air with cries of terror. They trampled over each other in the rush to reach lifeboats. Wave after wave thundered across the decks and the passengers climbed into the rigging to save themselves.

Captain Henry directed a boat lowered in order to get a line ashore through the wild breakers. The line would make a life-saving connection between ship and shore. However, once out in the seas, the crew of the boat cast off the line, abandoned the ship and rowed ashore. Likewise the second boat crew, despite the best and harshest entreaties of the captain and passengers, chopped the line and heartlessly turned their backs on the terrified passengers clinging to the rigging.

There were about two hundred persons on shore watching *New Era*, including ladies in carriages, surfmen or potential rescuers, wreckers, citizens, public officials and a Mr. Morris, the Coast Superintendent.

Hour after hour the desperate group on *New Era* shouted and raved, while lifesavers on shore tried to shoot a line across the wreck from a cannon. Many shots missed in the high wind, and several times the wire connected to the ball broke, but every time the cannon flashed, the trembling passengers cheered and groaned.

About noon, one shot fell across the middle of *New Era* and held fast. Soon a lifeboat was hauled from shore. Ten passengers climbed in, as well as the captain who was to help with bailing water, and pulled themselves by the rope toward the beach. Twice the boat upset, but it was finally drawn up on the sand with the captain and five other survivors who had clung to the keel.

WRECK OF THE OREGON UNDER PICKLECOMBE BATTERY,
PLYMOUTH SOUND 1867

When *New Era* stranded on the rocks on the New Jersey coast, there were nearly two hundred people on shore watching the drama unfold. As in this *Illustrated London News* drawing of March 30, 1867, a lifeline was established between the ship and rescuers on the beach.

Then the line to the wreck snapped. The lifesavers tried to shoot another line across the stranded vessel. All balls were used except the last and that caught in the main topsail brace. No one, crew or passengers, could reach it. The slender thread on which hundreds of lives depended hung there, but not a person stirred toward it. The cries of the passengers and the encouraging shouts of the lifesavers and wreckers on shore mixed with the roar of mountainous waves. Great combers shook the vessel and drove hundreds of terror-stricken men and women higher and higher into the fore, main and mizzen rigging.

Slowly and reluctantly the useless line was drawn back to the beach. The ship and passengers were beyond all earthly assistance and were abandoned through the following night.

In the morning seas and winds had abated somewhat. Those still alive were rescued, but 291 people died. One of those carried over the surf and dumped on the beach half-alive was a heavily pregnant woman, Amelia Donce. She gave birth to a son two hours after she reached the shore and both survived. However, the body of her husband washed in almost at her feet.

Many of the passengers were well-to-do, yet many could speak no English. It is said that two-thirds of the passengers had quantities of gold stitched in their underclothing. This enabled survivors to reach the American Midwest where they were bound as settlers.

# 7

## The eerie encounter of Ellen's captain

*September 1857*

For some reason, perhaps a navigational whim, the captain of the Norwegian barque *Ellen* changed course off the western Atlantic seaboard. He was not ordinarily a superstitious man, but as for what happened next the captain had no reasonable explanation. He said, "When I altered course a bird flew across the ship once or twice and then darted into my face. A few minutes later the bird repeated its movements. I thought this was an extraordinary thing and while thinking about it in this way, the mysterious bird reappeared and for the third time flew into my face. This induced me to alter my course back to the original one, and in a short time I heard noises in the sea and discovered that I was in the midst of shipwrecked people."

He said afterward (retold in the St. John's, Newfoundland, *Evening Herald* of November 14, 1893), "Who shall say what power guided the flight of the frail messenger, a bird, through the stormy air?" But, by whatever mysterious encounter, the *Ellen's* captain found forty-nine survivors of the wreck of S.S. *Central America*, which sank in a storm on September 12, 1857, about two hundred miles off the coast of South Carolina.

The great ship *Central America* was the 280-foot-long side-wheel mail steamship commanded by Captain William Lewis Herndon. He had guided the fortunes of people and their newly acquired riches aboard this ship from Panama north toward New York. The steamer carried nearly six hundred people, crew and passengers, many of whom were bringing back their personal stores of gold from the California Gold Rush. In addition, *Central America* carried $1.8 million in gold coins and bars belonging to the United States Treasury.

On September 5, it ran into a typical Atlantic storm. The ship began to leak. Captain Herndon asked the male passengers to form lines and pass the bailing buckets. Hour after hour the tempest howled and the huge vessel groaned as immense seas broke against her. All that time the ship's officers exhorted the bucket bailing gang not to pause for a moment if the ship were to be saved. Every passenger stuck to his post and worked until he fell to the deck exhausted. Then the women offered to take the places of their worn out, fainting husbands and brothers, but none of the men would allow it.

But as the horror of the situation gradually dawned on the minds of the women and children, the air was filled with sounds of terror. Above the roaring hurricane and the cries of panic came the chorus of the bucket men, chanting all day long: "Heave, ho! Heave, oh! Stamp and go, We'll be jolly blather, oh!"

A Mrs. Easton, a bride on her honeymoon trip on *Central America*, passed bottles of wine to the heroic men to strengthen them in their desperate work. All night long they struggled, but the ocean gained inch by inch. The women begged with tears in their eyes to be allowed to help. They cheered the brave fellows when they saw them fall to the deck, with white faces and trembling hands. Yet in the midst of it all, there were sailors and male passengers – some of great learning and high social standing – who deliberately became drunk and went to their berths. They stayed there raving until the seas swallowed them.

If the passengers thought things couldn't become worse, they were wrong. The next day food and water began to run out. The hurricane tossed the sinking hull, causing spars and a mast to shatter. While the men continued bailing, women knelt beside them, praying to God for assistance.

About two in the afternoon, a sail could be seen to the windward. The crew fired guns and flew signals of distress. The vessel, which turned out to be the brig *Marine* of Boston, answered the signals and tried to approach, but the wind blew it about three miles away.

*Central America*'s boats were prepared. Women and children steeled themselves to cross the mad seas to the waiting brig. To lessen their weight, they had to strip off nearly all clothes and don life preservers. Many of the women had gold in their clothes, which they could not carry with them into the lifeboat.

Two gold-bearing women went to the stateroom and took out bags of twenty-dollar gold pieces which they threw down in the cabin. Anyone would take what they wanted. The money rolled and jingled about the floor, while the two weeping women explained they would all be beggars if the ship was lost.

## DROWNED BY GOLD.

Preachers have seldom had a more scath-ing illustration of the deceitfulness of rich-es, and the overwhelming sacrifices that men and women will make for them, than is contained in the latest report from the Canary Isles, the scene of the awful disas-ter by which the "Sud-America" was sunk by collision with the French steamer "La France." Fifty bodies of the drown-ed still remain in their veritable "sleep-ing berths." A diver who has brought up several bodies reports that the vest of one man was simply lined with gold pieces, the value of which was between £500 and £600 sterling. The weight of the gold was such as to prevent the man from coming to the surface of the water, and was the sole cause of his being drowned The corpse of another man was encircled by a belt heavily weighted with specie. In the case of the body of a woman a large bag of gold was found in the breast of her clothing. These unfortunate passengers and probably many more were literally drowned by gold, of which they had no time to divest themselves. The authorities of the islands will not permit any more diving, and a salvage steamer is expected out shortly, when fresh discoveries will be made. The proceedings will necessarily be of a painful character, as the interment ac-commodation on the island is small, and the authorities have given orders that any fur-ther bodies shall be taken out to sea and sunk. But surely there is room for a com-mon grave, over which might be set a me-morial of this great disaster.—*Liverpool Post.*

THE DANGER OF GOLD

Many immigrants sold all they had, exchanged currency for gold and sewed the gold into their clothing. When a ship went down, the weight of gold towed its owner quickly under water. This clipping from the St. John's, Newfoiundland, *Evening Mercury* of October 30, 1888, tells the fate of some of the pasengers on *Sud-America* which sank near the Canary Islands.

The men stayed at their posts, saying they would remain on board until another ship arrived, as *Marine* would not be able to take them all. They insisted that the women and children had to be saved first. Among the heroes was the famous American minstrel and entertainer Billy Birch.

Two lifeboats had been smashed by the sea, but three boats were filled with women, children and babes in arms. The last boat to leave carried the second engineer. He solemnly promised Captain Herndon he would return with the boat, but the moment he got into the boat, he drew a knife and threatened to kill anyone who followed him.

Later on, when the women and children were put on board *Marine*, the engineer, like the coward and liar he was, refused to return. By now the sinking steamship was so low in the ocean almost every wave swept its deck. Some passengers climbed into the rigging; others tried to build a raft.

That night the storm continued to rage. The windblown *Marine* had disappeared beyond the horizon. *Central America* quivered and completely filled with water. The hosts of people left aboard clung to the decks and rigging, preparing for death. Many took loose pieces of wood and timber to construct crude rafts.

All at once the ship made a plunge and disappeared beneath the waves, taking its cargo of gold to the bottom. Nearly five hundred people were left to struggle in the fierce waves. To those who survived, the scenes of panic and horror were traumatic; some fainted at the mere retelling and the memory of it afterward. A few managed to hold on to debris all through the wild night. Many related stories of heroism, of Commander Herndon standing on the paddlewheel box as his ship went down under him.

Some also told of a miracle – the divine appearance of the barque *Ellen*, which came upon a mass of wreckage, scores of bodies and a few survivors. *Ellen* picked up forty-nine men; thus between the *Ellen* and *Marine* 149 people were rescued – thirty women, twenty-six children and ninety-three men. An estimated 425 died in the wreck of *Central America*.

Mrs. Easton survived, as did her husband. Despite being injured by debris, the San Francisco vaudevillian Billy Birch clung to a hatch window with several other men. He told his jokes and stories, keeping up the spirits until they were rescued.

The loss of the *Central America* and the several tons of gold it carried that were destined for east coast banks contributed to the Panic of 1857, an economic depression especially severe in the eastern states. This recession played a part in the impending Civil War.

The ship lay undisturbed under eight thousand feet of water for more than a hundred years. In 1985 Thomas G. Thompson of Columbus, Ohio, formed Columbus-America Discovery Group to find the ship and its valuable cargo, using new developments in sonar scanning and robotic technology to go where divers could not go. The salvagers eventually recovered a ton of gold bars and coins, sparking a lengthy court case between the salvors and the corporate heirs of the original insurers of the vessel and its contents. In 1995 American courts awarded the Columbus-America Discovery Group ninety percent of the salvage.

# 8

## Death of a pioneer sub

*February 1864*

Carrying a ninety-pound charge at the end of a seventeen-foot spar, the sub H.L. *Hunley* scored a direct hit on the U.S.S. *Housatonic* on a moonlit February night, sinking the ship in less than five minutes. Five on board the *Housatonic* died. But this was not a submarine of World War I vintage, but a Confederate Army submersible of the 1860s.

Late on the evening of February 17, 1864, the forty-foot-long H.L. *Hunley*, although not the first submersible developed by the United States, became the first submarine in history to sink an enemy surface ship during battle. It was a feat not duplicated until World War I.

Slipping beneath Union ships blockading Charleston harbour in South Carolina, *Hunley*'s crew maneuvered the sub to within feet of its prey. Then, with a few last cranks of its human-powered propeller, the *Hunley*'s crew rammed the *Housatonic* with a black powder explosive at the end of a pole. The detonation sent the *Housatonic* to the bottom minutes later.

Made from two locomotive boiler tanks, the sub demonstrated the advantage and danger of undersea warfare, for neither the *Hunley* nor any of its crew ever returned from the mission. After an extensive search, partially funded by novelist Clive Cussler, the sub, buried in silt, was discovered in 1995 off Charleston harbour. *H.L. Hunley* was almost intact and carried artifacts of its era and the remains of its crew.

# 9

## When the Evening Star went down

October 1866

One of the most terrible and unusual tragedies on the Atlantic coast was the loss of the steamship *Evening Star*. With 260 passengers and forty crew, the steamship left New York for New Orleans in September 1866. Included among the passengers were women, children and an Italian opera company. For several days the steamer rolled around in a constantly increasing storm.

At 1 o'clock in the morning of October 2, what was later described as "a vast mountain of water" fell on the deck, smashing the starboard forward gangway. The crew hastily erected a temporary bulkhead to keep the water out, but it was quickly swept away. Four times the crew rebuilt the wall, only to see the waves tear it away.

ORIENT LINE STEAMER CHIMBORAZO IN A GALE

A ship in heavy seas. Likewise *Evening Star*, pounded by wind and wave, was driven broadside onto a New Jersey beach. (*Illustrated London News*, February 21, 1880)

*Evening Star* began to list, the rudder was thrown out of gear and the sea made a clean breach over the ship. Crew, men and women passengers alike helped to bail the water out of the vessel, but the sea poured in relentlessly. There is an old Irish saying, "Fire and water have no mercy" and the captain realized this, saying there was little hope left for the *Evening Star* and those aboard. The captain asked all to be calm and to help bail out the ship. The members of the opera group and the prima donna herself worked at the buckets like the rest.

About dawn the next day the captain assembled the crew and passengers before him and solemnly addressed them. "This ship will go down soon!" he said and with those words, men and women panicked, rushing about the deck yelling, tearing off their clothes. Some jumped into the sea.

## When the Evening Star Went Down
## by Henry Clay Work

The morning was fearful at sea –
The voyagers weary and pale;
Their steamer a wreck, from keel to deck,
Before an Autumnal gale.
Old Neptune came forth in power--
He wore on his features a frown;
And many a guest he took to rest,
When the "Evening Star" went down.

They sleep in a fathomless grave,
The guest and the mariner brave;
They pillow their heads on coral beds,
Beneath the blue ocean waves,
Beneath the blue ocean waves.

Sail'd ever a ship from her quay,
So heavily laden as she,
With folly and fame, with hope and shame,
With vanity, mirth and glee?
But in the dark moment that came,
How useless were rank and renown!
And honors of earth, what were they worth,
When the "Evening Star" went down.

The treacherous ocean is calm--
No longer in storm billows toss'd;
Yet darkness and cloud will long enshroud
The hearts that were link'd with the lost.
In how many, how many homes,
Far distant, in country or town,
A light was put out, in dread, in doubt,
When the "Evening Star" when down.

Henry Clay Work (1832-1884), an American songwriter, printer and inventor, composed this song in 1866. He also penned "Grandfather's Clock" and "Marching Through Georgia."

*Evening Star* carried several lifeboats, but they could not be lowered in the towering waves. They remained on deck filled with people who waited for the ship to sink. They figured they would float off the deck when *Evening Star* went down. The captain wept and bade farewell to his companions.

In an hour the ship gave a lurch and plunged down into the ocean. The crowded lifeboats were sucked under, and the sea was full of men and women calling in vain for help. Scores of them were crushed by debris swirling around the wreck.

One of the last people seen on the ship before it sank was the prima donna, who waited calmly until all hope was gone. When she felt the first convulsion of the vessel, she raised her hand, moved her lips as if in prayer and fell into the roaring water, never to be seen again.

Seventeen were saved, but none of the opera troupe nor any women or children. The survivors drifted around, without food or drink, half mad with fear, until they were picked up by the Norwegian barque *Fleetwing*. They were transferred to the schooner *J. Waring* and on October 8 were taken to Savannah, Georgia.

# 10

## One survivor from the S.S. Cambria

October 1870

Many are the tales of immigrants who were shipwrecked on the shores of New England, Nova Scotia and Newfoundland, while sailing from the Old Country toward a new and better life in America. This is the story of a sole survivor, an immigrant who was sailing the opposite way – from New York to Ireland. His vessel was the S.S. *Cambria*, a 2,141-gross-ton ship with an overall length of 324 feet, three masts (rigged for sail) and an iron hull. It could reach a speed of twelve knots and could accommodate about 750 passengers.

Built by R. Duncan & Company, Port Glasgow, *Cambria* was launched for the Anchor Line in March 1869, but the great passenger ship made only twelve voyages. On October 19, 1870, it was wrecked with the loss of all aboard, 196 lives, except for one survivor, John McGartland.

The vessel, then under the command of Captain George Carnahan, struck the rocks on an island off Ireland, tearing a gash in its hull which flooded the engine room. Sailors lowered four boats, but the one containing sixteen people capsized. Of that number only John McGartland was picked up by the steamer *Enterprise.* The other boats drifted away in the darkness and were never found.

Recently, McGartland's recollections of the wreck and his story of survival became known. "I was in America twelve months," he said, "but on October 8, 1870, I sailed in steerage [the lowest passenger class] from New York for the Old Country. The weather was calm at first and we all expected a fine voyage."

Conditions quickly changed, McGartland recalled, to a high wind with a troubled sea. A gale increased so that by Wednesday night, October 19, the wind was "furious." Heavy rain fell, and waves broke over the sides of the steamer. McGartland stayed on deck till about eleven o'clock when he went below and lay in his bunk, thinking of old times and his near approach to home. He remembered: "Suddenly there was a horrid crash and I went spinning forward on my face to the floor. I did not lose my senses although I was a great deal frightened and, getting to my feet, hurried back up to the deck. Here I found passengers running to and fro in great excitement, but I cannot say there was much crying or shouting.

"I heard the order given, 'Launch the boats!' I cannot say whose voice it was. I also heard someone say, 'There's a mighty big hole in the ship.'

"Our vessel, I now know, had struck the rock at Inishtrahull Island, Donegal. But at that time I really saw nothing beyond the boat itself – the night was so dark and there was so much blinding rain and spray. Sometime before the wreck I saw two lights, but I did not know the Irish coast and can't say where or what the lights were.

RESCUE OF ELEVEN PERSONS FROM THE SHIP ALARM OF BELFAST
BY A LIFEBOAT IN BALLYCOTTON BAY

In 1866, when the *Alarm* was lost, a lifeboat stayed upright and eleven people survived, said the *Illustrated London News* of April 14, 1866. With the S.S. *Cambria* four years later, sixteen climbed into a boat, but when it capsized John McGartland lived.

"There were seven small boats on board, but four were lowered. One of them was in the forepart of the ship; the others were in the cabin end of the ship. I did not see these in the water and I knew nothing of their fate. When the boat in the steerage end was lowered I got into it with others."

This was the beginning of a near-death experience for John McGartland. He recalled that there were ten or eleven other steerage passengers in the boat as well as two seamen from the *Cambria*. No provisions had been taken on board as they were very near shore.

54

McGartland describes what happened: "Our boat was scarcely launched when it capsized. When it lurched over I got hold of it, but I cannot say what part of it. When it righted again I managed to scramble in. I never saw a living soul after that. I did not hear a single cry when the boat heeled over and I never afterwards saw any of my companions.

"I was tossed about, but must have grabbed the boat mechanically and when I got into it again I don't know that I could have told exactly where I was. I didn't see the *Cambria* go down, as the waves carried my boat quickly away from it.

"When I recovered my senses, I noticed someone lying in the bottom of the lifeboat. I stooped down and found it was a young woman, lying face downward. She was dead. The body was dressed in a black silk gown, but I didn't pay attention to anything else. I think she was a steerage passenger going to some place between Inniskillen and Irvinestown. Nothing could be done for her and I didn't feel able to do much for myself. The oars were tied with small ropes to the boat and I was not equal to the exertion of recovering them. I just let the boat drift aimlessly along.

"The wind and waves carried me all morning with my melancholy burden – the poor thing in the bottom of the boat. After daybreak the wind moderated somewhat and the rain slackened. The sea continued to run high; waves lashed over my boat and every moment I expected it to go down."

McGartland concludes his tale of survival, saying, "I knew no more than the dead where I was or where I was drifting to." At half past twelve the next afternoon, or nearly fifteen hours after *Cambria* went down, he was still adrift, nearly drowned and suffering from exposure in the cold October wind and rain.

The single lifeboat was seen by Captain Gillespie of the steamer *Enterprise*. The dying McGartland was not even able to signal for help. Sailors got a rope around his body, and he was pulled to the deck of the steamer and eventually carried to Londonderry. The sole survivor was confined to bed for several days. "I lost all my clothes and eleven guineas in money," he said. "Beside that, a brother of mine in America entrusted me with parcels of goods to friends and relatives at home, but all these have been lost."

# 11

## Too weak to eat flour

*October 1872*

The schooner *Seriole* sailed from Liverpool, Nova Scotia, on August 8, 1872, bound for Demerara, British Guyana (George-town, Guyana). It had a partial load of general supplies, flour and other consumables. No doubt its intended cargo was the light cane sugar or the dark rum Demerara is famous for.

However, no sooner was the ship off the coast of Nova Scotia when a typical fall hurricane pounced. *Seriole* was thrown on its beam ends – on its side with masts and sails nearly parallel to the water – and the captain, seeing no immediate prospect of the ship righting itself, ordered the masts cut away. In the windstorm the vessel was unmanage-able, seas broke over the wreck constantly and the seven-man crew were exposed to the elements. There was no way to get below deck, not even to reach any food and water that was not contaminated by salt water.

On August 31, the storm abated. With the seas and waves less treacherous on the following day, the men were able to move about the ship more and succeeded in breaking a hole through the deck. It was just wide enough to admit the arm of a seaman, who reached down and pulled up a small quantity of flour from an open barrel. Moistening the flour somewhat made it palatable. It was the only food they had tasted since *Seriole* had become a sea-wracked hulk some days previously. By then, the captain and another seaman, Lewis W. Leather, were too weak and overcome by exposure to eat even flour.

On September 2, one of the men caught some small fish and the crew ate them raw, first sucking the blood from them to quench their raging thirst. Despite their best efforts, they could only catch one or two fish after fishing all day. This meagre fare, moistened flour and a few raw fish, was the only nourishment they had until Thursday, September 5, when a sea turtle came alongside the vessel. It was captured and the blood and flesh divided equally. By this time the captain, the cook and Leather were delirious.

The next day, the crew managed to collect two cups of rain water when they spread oil cloths on deck. This was enough to moisten their lips and tongues and provided precious little drinking water. On the Sunday morning following, Leather died. The captain fell unconscious and continued in that condition until the 11th when he too passed away.

The survivors remained on the wreck until September 15, enduring agony from hunger, thirst and exposure, until they felt at the end of their limits. On that day the brig *Eliza Stevens*, out of Boston, happened to see the derelict, came by and rescued the remaining crew. The cook died a few hours after he was transferred to the brig; the others were carried to Martinique. However, the last four survivors recovered through the careful treatment from Captain Sears and his crew.

# 12

## One of the most frightful wrecks

*April 1873*

The news of a great wreck came on what is termed today April Fool's Day. And that's how the newspapers regarded the terrible report at first – an attempt to perpetrate a cruel April Fool hoax. At 2 a.m. on April 1, 1873, the White Star steamship *Atlantic* struck Meagher's (or Mosher's) Island, a few miles south of Halifax, Nova Scotia. Five hundred and sixty-two perished out of a total of 952 persons.

Launched November 26, 1870, the 3,700-ton *Atlantic* was the second White Star ship to serve on the transatlantic run, after its sister ship *Oceanic*. On its maiden run in 1871, *Atlantic* made its eastward trip from New York to Liverpool in ten days. The ship's accommodations were luxurious. The fixed chairs of the lounge were upholstered in red velvet, and the walls were white and pink. Parts of the ship were decorated in gold and each cabin had running water. One passenger even commented, "We have a host of little comforts, some of which are not to be had in a first-class Swiss hotel."

Seven watertight compartments would be useless, however, if the great ship ran upon rocks. Captain James Agnew Williams' intended destination was America, but a shortage of coal and a storm forced him to head to Halifax. Ship's officers miscalculated speed and distance and without the slightest warning and at nearly full speed the steamer struck on the rock. The sea carried away all the port-side boats. Before the boats on the weather side could be cleared, the ship rolled over. The sounds that arose from between decks were piteous or as one newspaper of the day described it, "soul-stirring." Most of the women and children were down there in darkness wailing.

Captain Williams ordered the passengers to climb into the rigging and to crowd forward where the wreck was highest and out of reach of the waves. Three of the more courageous of *Atlantic*'s crew decided to swim ashore. Quartermaster George Speakman carried a line with him to Mosher's Island and he was followed by Third Officer Brady and Quartermaster Owens. The three, by means of a line, hauled a heavier hawser ashore, set up a breeches buoy, and began transferring people from the ship to shore. Several passengers drowned in the attempt.

Quartermaster Robert Thomas and an unknown passenger swam to the village of Lower Prospect and called for help. Learning that help was on the way, Brady made a sign "Cheer up, the boats are coming!" and held it up for Captain Williams to see.

After awhile about two hundred people managed to reach a small rock, barely awash. Between this rock and the shore was a gulf of about three hundred feet. Several people reached the village of Prospect and aroused the inhabitants, who furnished boats to take the half frozen survivors from the rocks.

AN INCIDENT AT THE WRECK OF THE S.S. ATLANTIC

Not one woman was saved from the wreck, although a seaman held the lifeless body of one, thinking there was life. (A sketch by Charles Kendrick in the *Canadian Illustrated News*, April 5, 1873)

Meanwhile, the tides lowered and about five a.m. the stern was left unsupported. The hull broke, and the stern then sank into the sea. The water washed the women and children out of steerage. No woman survived, although the first officer held one woman in the rigging until she froze to death. There she was left half nude, with protruding eyes and foamy lips – a sight made more terrible by the splendid jewels that sparkled on her hands.

Almost all were taken off by 8:40 a.m. except for a young boy, John Hindley, and First Officer John Firth. They were still clinging to the wreck and the sea made it impossible for rescue craft to come near. The Anglican minister, Reverend William Ancient of Terence Bay/Prospect, decided to take matters into his own hands. He and a volunteer crew

The marble plaque dedicated to the loss of the S.S. *Atlantic* at Prospect, Nova Scotia, has inscribed ". . . April 1st 1873 when 562 persons perished, of whom 277 were interred in this churchyard . . ." (Photo by Robert C. Parsons)

rowed for the *Atlantic* but could not board. As their boat came around, Hindley lost his hold and fell into the water. Ancient pulled him to safety. Ancient then took a rope and threw it to Firth, who wrapped it around himself before jumping ship. Ancient then pulled him to safety too. Hindley was the only child to survive.

Captain Williams, who survived the wreck, was heard to remark that he would have given his life if only one woman had survived. The Clancy family of Prospect, like scores of others, cared for, sheltered, fed and clothed survivors, many of whom knew no one in the land and had lost what scant worldly goods they once possessed.

News of the disaster did not reach Halifax until 5:30 p.m., after Third Officer Brady had walked to Halifax to deliver the message himself. At first many thought it was an April Fool's joke, but they soon realized that the story was no jest.

# 13

## Capsized on its maiden voyage

April 1876

The banking schooner *Henrietta Greenleaf* was a new vessel. When it left Gloucester, Massachusetts, on Thursday, April 6, 1876, the schooner sailed on its first trip – and its last. The captain and part owner was William H. Greenleaf. The schooner *Lizzie K. Clark* rescued him and four others, out of a crew of fifteen.

On Friday evening, *Henrietta Greenleaf* reached a spot south of LaHave Bank and had clear fine weather. The wind was coming up, a six-knot south-southwest breeze, when the watch changed at twelve midnight. George Olsen and Philip McCloud stood watch; the others were below asleep.

Around 3 a.m. one of the watch called all hands to handle sail, and most men had reached the deck. The wind had come up suddenly. Captain Greenleaf took the wheel and just as he did, the schooner listed out. The sails and masts went down parallel to the water. The captain said it was the most intense squall he had ever experienced and it came so suddenly there was no escape from it.

Greenleaf shouted for all to go to the weather side. "Get out the axes. Chop away the rigging. Let the masts and sails go over the side!"

Getting rid of the masts would ease the strain on the vessel and it might right itself. It was no use. It was evident *Henrietta Greenleaf* was sinking and the crew could only save their lives if they got off the vessel as soon as possible. There was no time even to snatch oars, water, or food. Only the two men on watch were adequately dressed; the others had only pants, shirts and shoes or rubbers on – no oilskins. Even so, it required great effort to get two dories over the side.

As they worked feverishly, the captain made a quick muster of the crew. Four were missing, and it could only be presumed they had been unable to reach the deck because of the great flood of water pouring down through the companionway. Unaccounted for were the captain's brother, Franklin Greenleaf, age twenty-five; Alfred Short, of Norway; James Peters, Prospect, Nova Scotia; and fifteen-year-old George Connors, the brother-in-law of Captain Greenleaf. The loss of these four naturally dominated the minds and hearts of the remaining crew, but they couldn't feel despondent at that time. They had to work together and quickly. Half an hour after *Henrietta Greenleaf* went on its beam ends, they pushed the dories off from the side of the vessel.

Winds were high, the sea choppy, but the two dories kept together all day Saturday. Toward the end of the day came snow squalls, sleet and low temperatures. The eleven survivors were wet with flying spray or water shipped by the dories, which required constant bailing. They had no oars and pulled off the inside railings of the dories to use as oars. One dory also had the wheel box from *Henrietta Greenleaf*, which had torn away when it sank, and the boards from this made makeshift paddles. Thus the men were able to maneuver the head of the dories into the wind and were able to keep the little crafts afloat.

At 8 p.m. Saturday in a strong north-northwest wind, the dories drifted apart. Aboard one were Joseph Gardner of Liverpool, Nova Scotia; George Rowe, East Gloucester; Bernard Jewett and Charles Pattie, both of Westport, Maine; and John S. Tobbie of Norway. The other had the captain and five men.

The wind kept up until Sunday noon when it moderated. At five in the afternoon Freeman Crawford, in the second dory, succumbed to exposure and fatigue. He was also from Westport. By now the remaining men were beginning to think if they were not rescued soon, they would perish. Shortly after midnight Monday morning they saw a sail approaching. Somehow they attracted the attention of those on the vessel. When it came near, they recognized the *Lizzie K. Clark* of Gloucester, the home port of *Henrietta Greenleaf*. Within a few minutes Captain Thomas Hodgdon and his crew responded to the cries and shouts from a drifting dory. To their surprise the castaways were men they knew and who sailed out of the same port.

The men were lifted aboard carefully, fed and warmed. Captain Hodgdon stayed in the general area all day Monday, sailing about, cruising in various directions, trying to spot the other dory. It was nowhere to be seen. The rescued men had to have medical attention and the captain left for Halifax, the nearest port. He arrived on Tuesday and the survivors were hospitalized.

At Halifax *Henrietta Greenleaf*'s remaining crew received attention: money, clothing, sympathy and a free ride by steamer to Portland, Maine, then by train to Massachusetts. Surviving the wreck were Captain Greenleaf, Lawrence Hardiman, Philip McCloud and the two men who were on watch when *Henrietta Greenleaf* capsized. Those in the other dory were never heard from again.

# 14

## The end of the N.W. Blethen

*July 1876*

Two years. A few voyages. One disastrous storm and the great wooden ship *N.W. Blethen* was gone. Built in 1874 for Dennis and Doane of Yarmouth, Nova Scotia, the 1,092-ton sailing vessel left Baltimore on July 25, 1876, for London with a cargo of corn. Captain Cox had his wife and two children with him; his mate was Frederick W. Blethen, son of a prominent Yarmouth resident after whom the ship was named.

The *Blethen*, as it was commonly called, ran into high winds around 3 a.m. of July 31, so intense the captain called up the watch and all hands clewed up and furled the upper topsail, the mizzen lower topsail and the fore topmast stay sail. Just before daylight with the wind still increasing, the foresail was clewed and mate James C. Doty and some sailors went aloft to furl it.

Doty and his men inched their way out onto the yard, holding on with one arm and furling sail with the other and probably repeating the old sailor's saying, "One arm for the ship, one arm for yourself."

Just as mate Doty reached the yard, a powerful wind knocked the ship over, throwing it onto its beam ends. The cargo of corn shifted and the vessel remained listed out. The mate and his crew were called down to help get the vessel back on an even keel.

After the whole crew worked the rigging and sails and hove the wheel up, the *Blethen* leveled off slightly, enough that the crew succeeded in getting the vessel before the wind. By now the *Blethen* had shipped a lot of water on the decks and as the list was still severe, it laboured heavily.

At that moment a great sea struck the *Blethen* on the port side and this righted it somewhat. However, just as Captain Cox, mate Doty and the tired seamen thought the worst was over, a terrific and intense squall of wind struck the ship. Sails were blown from the yards, the cargo shifted again, and once more N.W. *Blethen* fell over on its side. This time the consequences were catastrophic.

Captain Cox stood on the weather quarter; his wife and children were in the cabin. At the instant the ship heeled over, the captain was washed along the deck. He managed to grab the wheel, but could not hold on and went over the side. He called out to those on the side of the ship, "Men, we are gone!" and was seen no more. In that moment of looking out for and trying to help the doomed captain, the rest of the seamen relaxed their concentration, perhaps not gripping lifelines or rigging securely. In that instant a great comber washed over the vessel and carried all standing on deck into the sea.

H.M.S. WYVERN IN A HEAVY SEA IN THE CHANNEL

When the *N.W. Blethen* shipped heavy seas, it listed out. FInally, water filled the holds and the ship fell over on one side. Three people survived out of twenty-one. Most vessels that were watertight when seas poured over the decks made it through the storm, as did H.M.S. *Wyvern*, shown here in the English Channel. (*Illustrated London News*, October 27, 1866)

Mate Doty was one of three who lived to tell the tale. He said after: "I came to the surface of the water and got hold of a plank. Seeing the ship's boy close to me, I called to the boy to come with me and we succeeded on getting another plank to support us.

"Looking around, I saw the ship bottom up and the men going down one after another, but could render them no assistance. After being on the planks for about three hours, I saw a man drifting towards me, apparently on a raft. This proved to be the top of the *Blethen*'s after house. The boy and

I succeeded in getting on this and with the spanker down-haul ropes, we lashed ourselves to this piece of wreckage.

"After we drifted in this condition for fifty-six hours without food or water, a ship hove in sight and headed for us. Its crew threw lines and hauled us on board. It was the barque *C.E. Jaynes* of New York, Captain Osborne. They had on board one of our men whom they had picked up a short time before."

Out of twenty-one souls on board *N.W. Blethen*, the boy and two seamen were saved, while the rest of the crew, the captain and his whole family perished.

# 15

## So close, yet so far away

At first, the news that there were lives lost to the age-less nemesis, the sea, seemed impossible. But it was true – twenty-eight lives were gone in an instant. The oddity of it all was that *Circassian* went to pieces within sight of a highly populated area, while a salvage crew was on board the derelict to make it secure.

*Circassian*, a name derived from a region in the Caucasus Mountains, was a large iron-hulled ship: 1,741 tons, 280 feet long and 39 feet wide. It had three masts, all iron, and carried full sail. Including the captain and three apprentices, it had a crew of thirty-five men. The ship's command on this voyage was assigned to an able young Welshman, Captain Richard Williams.

On December 11, 1876, in heavy weather, *Circassian* went aground on Long Island, New York, two miles south of the village of Bridgehampton, west of the Mecox Life Saving Station. All the crew were taken off the stranded ship by shore-based lifesaving personnel.

The ship lay on its side for more than two weeks. At first, it was deemed a salvaging company could free the ship from its position and, later in December, salvagers put workers aboard. *Circassian*'s Captain Williams and some of his sailors had already gone back aboard so the salvaging company would not have an abandoned ship to claim. Williams' men could also help move cargo and keep the vessel shipshape. Also aboard were some native Americans, Shinnecock Indians from a nearby reservation, who were employed to remove cargo and to lighten the ship. All told, there were thirty-two people aboard *Circassian*.

Salvagers finished work aboard *Circassian* on the night of December 29, and made everything ready for a heavy hawser with which the stranded ship would be pulled from its position. At daylight work would be completed. However, during the early hours of the morning the wind freshened a little and the sea began to run high, with six-foot waves. That was enough to stop work. But the sea is unpredictable and soon waves pounded the beached ship, eventually making a clean breach, sweeping completely over the vessel.

To prevent anyone from being carried overboard, all were ordered to the foremast and rigging. That position became dangerous when some of the foretop rigging began to fall due to the rolling of the vessel. All transferred to the mizzenmast; this time, they ran up signals of distress to those on the shore.

WRECK OF THE STEAMSHIP EARL PERCY AT TYNEMOUTH

When the *Circassian* went aground in December 1876, it too was near land. When waves washed over its deck in a sudden storm, salvagers and some of its crewmen were forced to the rigging. They perished within sight of watchers on shore. The *Illustrated London News* of February 11, 1865, shows a similar situation with the *Earl Percy* at Tynemouth, England.

Throughout the ordeal, the shoreline was in plain sight, the moon shone and generally conditions appeared normal, except on *Circassian* where waves breaking over the deck had forced thirty-two people to the rigging. The lifesaving crew on shore built a fire and those on the ship could see crowds of people gathered on the beach to watch the drama unfold.

Yet it was terrible suspense to the stranded men. They saw attempt after attempt made to reach them fail. There was no way to get a boat off; great combers drove each craft back high and dry on the beach.

Henry Hunting, captain of the lifesaving station, brought a mortar (a rope-firing cannon) into service. Several balls with rope attached were shot to the ship. With the wind blowing a gale from the direction in which the balls were shot, only one rope reached the vessel. Its hold was not firm or it slipped back into the sea.

In agony and suspense the early morning wore on. The wind swung around west-southwest. Before the men had taken to the rigging aboard *Circassian*, the cables securing the vessel to the shore were slackened. Often the ship lifted up and pounded down on the bottom; every time it struck, the men thought the masts would go over the side. All realized the danger and the impossibility of saving themselves.

At 4:30 a.m. the inevitable happened – the ship broke apart into three pieces. The mizzenmast went down with a crush, carrying the mainmast with it. Some men, less securely lashed to the mast and rigging, were swept away; others perished when the iron masts went under water.

When it was over, four survived. Among *Circassian's* crew and the wrecking company men lost were Captain T. Richard Williams, third mate Evan Johnson, bosun Keepp, steward Horatio Johnson and several other crewmen and apprentices. Ten victims were the native American employees of the wrecking company.

Three of those saved were *Circassian* seamen: first mate Henry Morle, second mate John Rowland, and Alexander Wilson, the ship's carpenter. Also listed among the survivors was Charles Campbell, an engineer with the wrecking company.

# 16

## *A sudden and tremendous shock*

*February 1877*

*A*bout two o'clock on the morning of February 7, 1877, the Italian barque *Bozzo* was steaming from London to Baltimore. Off New Haven, Connecticut, *Bozzo* encountered fog and choppy seas. The ship continued at reduced speed, but soon was running in heavier seas. Fog conditions were described as "so dense that a vessel's lights could only be seen at a short distance."

Without any warning *Bozzo* received a sudden and tremendous shock. Its bowsprit, foremast and mainmast broke off and fell over the side, tearing away the rigging. Debris from the top hamper – sail, blocks, ropes, yards – came crashing down on deck.

It was determined later that a French vessel had struck *Bozzo*, then split in two and sank immediately, carrying down four of its crew. Three were saved when they caught loose

THE LACONIA RESCUING THE CREW OF THE AMALIA
IN THE BAY OF BISCAY

On February 7, 1877, the *Embla* sent boats over to the *Bozzo* to take off the crew. In this image from the *Illustrated London News*, January 27, 1866, *Laconia's* sailors in lifeboats attempt to pluck crew from the sinking *Amalia*.

rigging hanging down over the side of *Bozzo* and were pulled up over the side by the Italian crew.

*Bozzo* didn't sink immediately, but water rose so fast in the holds that its crew determined it had to go down soon. Yet they kept at the pumps, ran up distress signals and sounded the foghorn at intervals.

At 6:30 the same morning the *Embla*, under Captain Sorensen's command, sailed in the general vicinity en route from Hull, England, to New York. Sorensen and crew, hearing the fog signals from the distressed Italian ship, eventually edged down closer to the wreck.

*Bozzo* lay in the trough of the sea, utterly helpless and rolling heavily, its gunwale only a foot or so from sea level. Seas swept its decks continuously. *Bozzo's* boats were entangled in the rigging that had fallen over the hatches and cabin.

Yet, despite these trying circumstances, the crew managed to free a boat. *Bozzo's* entire crew, the fourteen men sent over from *Embla* and the three rescued from the French vessel were saved. Rescuers and rescued had just reached *Embla's* side when the stricken Italian ship lurched leeward with an unusually heavy roll. A flood of water poured over its deck and, borne down with the extra weight, the vessel never righted again. It sank within a minute.

*Bozzo's* crew, plus the three unexpected passengers, landed at New Haven on February 9, two days after the collision.

# 17

## Sole survivor of the brig Roanoke

*March 1877*

Captain Carson of the schooner *Addie Todd* saw something unusual in the early morning of March 27, 1877. He marked his position – latitude 38.20, longitude 70.30 – in the log book and picked up his telescope to look again.

It seemed to be a ship, or a section of a ship, showing distress signals and he tacked *Addie Todd* over for a closer look. "I found it was a part of a wreck," he said. "On passing close to it, I saw two men calling for assistance. It was blowing heavily at the time with a high sea running, and no assistance could be rendered."

But Captain Carson didn't give up easily. An unwritten code of the sea says that if a ship or sailor needs help, you give it. Like all fishermen and mariners, he knew only too well the demands and claims of the relentless ocean, and believed as well a rescue favour might someday be returned.

Carson laid to until the weather moderated and four hours later the gale abated slightly. His crew put up some sail and beat back to the vessel. "We passed close aboard and found that one of the two men had died. We threw lines to the wreck which the surviving man failed to catch."

After several attempts, finally, about two in the afternoon, the man on the wreck caught a line and was hauled on board the *Addie Todd*. He was barely alive, but once revived, told his story.

He was William McGuire. He had left Philadelphia on the brig *Roanoke* on Sunday afternoon, March 18. Captain Wilkie was in command with his crew of nine and three passengers – Mr. and Mrs. Dallett and a Spanish gentleman bound for Porto Cabello, Venezuela. *Roanoke* also had aboard general cargo and mail destined for Jamaica. On Monday afternoon a westerly gale came on and Wilkie had the sails shortened until twelve midnight. *Roanoke* became difficult to steer and broached to, or drifted side-on to the high winds, and shipped a heavy sea which filled the decks.

As McGuire recalled: "We failed to get the vessel before the wind and we had to cut the mainmast away. This fell on the deck, breaking the cabin and damaging the deck. The foremast was then cut away. The forward house and booby hatches let the sea in and our ship was nearly filled with water, leaving it entirely unmanageable. All hands and passengers then got aft on the quarterdeck with the seas still making a clean breach across the main deck."

By daybreak Tuesday, March 20, winds were southerly, still at gale force. The lookout saw a sail and at 9 a.m. it could be seen that a schooner was in the distance. The unidentified schooner ran down near the storm-racked *Roanoke* and Wilkie ran up distress signals. But to the utter disgust of all, it continued on its course. McGuire said afterward, "Had the vessel laid by us, it could have probably saved all hands."

CUTTING AWAY THE MASTS

An expression in ink in the *Illustrated London News*, November 6, 1880, showing sailors – as they did on the *Roanoke* – using an axe to save their lives. When a ship listed out on its side, the weight of masts and sails sometimes kept the vessel in that position. Sometimes it came upright when masts were cut down.

After that bitter disappointment, *Roanoke*'s complement got out the preserved food and some lager beer which was part of the cargo. Weather improved somewhat on Wednesday. A barque was spotted to the leeward, but the passing ship did not see the *Roanoke*. As if to pile on the agony, that evening another severe gale came on from the northwest and seas became heavy.

McGuire said, "Thursday the 22nd, the seas broke clean over the fore and aft of the vessel. By this time the captain wished to take to the boats to save life, but he was persuaded not to do it.

"In the afternoon Mr. and Mrs. Dallett were exhausted. They shook hands with the captain and mate and bade them good-bye, expressing the hope they would all meet again in heaven. Mr. Dallett took his wife's waterproof coat, wrapped it around her head, and they embraced each other. Without the strength to hold on, a sea swept them overboard and they drowned. The Spanish gentleman shortly followed. He said his prayers, wrapped a quilt around his head and leaped overboard in a delirious state.

"Shortly after this a sea carried away the afterdeck. The captain, steward, one sailor and a boy were on it. They drifted away with it and were seen no more. The stern broke away and went next with the mate and second mate. The mate perished nearly alongside the *Roanoke*, but the second mate was on a piece of the stern when last seen."

By then only William McGuire and two other men were left. Suffering horribly from thirst, they lashed themselves onto the stump of the mainmast. A brig passed close but, as if taunting the flagging spirits of the three, it did not stop. Unable to get below to get food, they were reduced to eating tallow, or animal fat. There was no water and raging thirst became their greatest enemy.

The gale continued all Friday and they saw another ship, a barque, which like the previous vessels did not stop. The next day weather improved; the sun came out. With some hope, the three found some candles and a tin of sardines, but no water. McGuire said, "On Sunday, March 25, the wind came on again, blowing a gale from the northeast. One man became crazed from thirst and jumped overboard. The next day there was some rain with the wind, but the sea was breaking over the ship so that we could not get much rainwater to drink.

"At daylight Tuesday, we saw a schooner which later proved to be the *Addie Todd*. I made signals and it lay to, but it blew too hard for it to assist us. When the gale lulled, it bent back to our wreck and after trying five times, I succeeded in catching a line and was hauled on board. While the *Addie Todd* was lying to, another man became crazed and leaped overboard."

Thus sole survivor William McGuire ended his epic: eight of nine crew and three passengers perished. McGuire was landed at Boston on April 2.

# 18

## Simply, a miraculous rescue

The first reports reaching shore said there were only three survivors from the fishing vessel *Codseeker* – the captain and two crewmen. They saved themselves in a dory, but ten other men were not accounted for.

While fishing off Cape Sable Island, Nova Scotia, the *Codseeker* was struck by heavy seas on Wednesday, May 9, 1877. About 11 p.m. the schooner gradually careened over on its beam ends in which position, listed out on one side, it remained.

The crew worked but found the task of freeing the ship's life dory or any of its fishing dories imposible, except one which floated off the capsized vessel. Captain Brown and two men reached this craft and, while trying to keep it from turning over in choppy seas, bailed for their lives. They drifted away to the leeward, leaving some of the crew clinging to the side of the schooner. These men had been on deck working the sails when *Codseeker* went over, but three or four other men had been below, probably asleep, and thus likely drowned. Another man could not be accounted for and was probably in the hold of the schooner.

After a tremendous struggle with the seas and surf, the three survivors landed in the breakers on the south side of Cape Sable Island. It was daylight, May 10. They found some people who were living on the island and eventually acquired the services of a schooner. In the face of a great gale, they went to the scene of *Codseeker*'s last known location.

Twelve hours after the accident, *Codseeker* was sighted still on its beam ends with five of its crew lashed to the side. One of the crew had washed off during the night and perished before he could be reached. One died on the side of the ship just before help reached him; the other four were rescued. The rest were presumed dead, as they were trapped below when the vessel went over. The hulk of what was once a fine fishing schooner was abandoned to its fate. No doubt this rescue of four survivors in itself was a thrilling tale of the sea, but what happened a day or so later is even more inspiring.

On Sunday noon May 12, three and a half days after the tragedy, crew aboard the Bucksport, Maine, schooner *Ohio* saw a wrecked vessel off Seal Island. The captain and two seamen boarded the overturned derelict. To their amazement, they thought they heard sounds coming from the forecastle area. They dismissed it as fancy, thinking, "No, it couldn't be! There's no one alive aboard this hulk." But faint knocks from the companionway area of the forecastle made them hesitate. The gangway – the stairway to the forecastle – was completely under water.

The *Ohio* men pounded on the side of the vessel; faint tappings from within answered. They conclued that someone

The crew from the schooner *Ohio* used axes or saws to get into the hold of the capsized *Codseeker*, rescuing two men who had been trapped for nearly four days. (Sketch by Andrea Hatch)

must have been caught in the forecastle and imprisoned when the vessel capsized.

At once they went back to their own ship, found saws or axes and returned to the derelict. They cut a hole in the side of the schooner by the fore chains and pulled out two men – James E. Smith and Samuel Atwood – who had indeed been trapped inside the hull of their own vessel. By the time they were rescued it was 4 o'clock Sunday evening.

For almost four days, eighty-nine hours, they had existed without light, water, or food, with the exception of a few small cakes of ship's biscuit. There had been three trapped, but one, William A. Smith, perished from cold, exposure and terror or shock.

James Smith and Atwood were landed in their homes – probably Port Clyde, Bear Point or another southern Nova Scotian port – on Monday morning to the great joy of their families and friends, who had given them up for lost. Needless to say, while William Smith's family were happy for the survivors, they grieved the loss of a father and husband.

Who can express the feelings of these men in their long and apparently hopeless confinement? Who knows what despair must have weighted their souls and darkened their minds when their comrades were taken from the wreck on Thursday, leaving them without means of making their presence known.

In the tomblike hole of the forecastle, they cheered themselves up in the long hours after and then they went through intense anxiety when they became aware that their vessel was boarded again on Sunday afternoon. How could they express their joy when they knew their signals had been heard and their deliverance was at hand?

*Codseeker* was eventually towed into Barrington, Nova Scotia, where the body of another dead seaman, Robert Barss, was removed from the hold. The fishing schooner was repaired and lived to sail again. Later it was sold to a fishing business in Newfoundland.

---

*Survivors of wreck of Codseeker, May 9, 1877*

Captain Philip Brown
Nat Knowles
John Smith

*Survivors rescued from the side of Codseeker, May 10*

William E. Kenney
William Goodwin
Jesse Smith
Jeremiah Nickerson

*Lost from the side of Codseeker*

Ziba Hunt
Ansel Crowell Nickerson

*Drowned in the hold*

Robert Barss

*Perished in the forecastle*

William A. Smith

*Found alive aboard Codseeker, Sunday, May 12*

James E. Smith
Samuel Atwood

# 19

## Mutiny on a Halifax brig

It was not always easy to get hardworking, reliable seamen to handle canvas in the era of all-sail ships. The best – knowledgeable and experienced able-bodied seamen and dependable deck hands – readily found work, but when a ship became shorthanded, it was often necessary to take someone less than desirable. Desperate captains and owners with busy shipping schedules often had to take whoever the dregs of society offered up.

This became all too real for Captain Howard on the Nova Scotia brig *George S. Berry*. A little after midnight on November 1, 1879, he found himself facing two mobsters. His life and ship were spared when help came from an unexpected source.

Howard was bound from Pensacola on Florida's Pan-handle to Montevideo, Uruguay. In addition to his regular crew the captain's eighteen-year-old daughter Ida sailed with him, perhaps as an excursion, a holiday to southern climes. She was described by all as a beautiful tall girl, intelligent and refined. She certainly had courage and determination in heroic quantities, as her father was soon to find out.

At Pensacola Captain Howard shipped a new crew, except the mate, to replace sailors who had left the vessel for some obscure reason. Among the new hands were seamen Thomas Britt and another named Welch. After *George S. Berry* left port it made good time in fine sailing weather. About 10 or 11 o'clock on the night of November 1, Ida Howard had retired for the night and was asleep in the cabin.

As the ship approached the Tortugas Islands off the southwest coast of Florida, Captain Howard was on deck, the mate was at the wheel and other seamen were aloft. The mate had to go forward to help with some ship duty and gave Britt the wheel. Seaman Welch came up from down below. While the captain was walking about the deck, Welch crept up behind him. Both Welch and Britt had one common goal – mutiny, to take control of the *George S. Berry* – and, at that moment, saw their opportunity to attack the unarmed captain.

Without warning, Welch stabbed Captain Howard in the back, inflicting a deep, but not fatal, wound. Howard was able to turn on his attacker and attempted to wrest the knife from him. He may have done so, but at that moment Britt left the wheel and also swung his knife at the captain, saying, "Now then, knife him good."

Before the mate and the sailors aloft knew what was happening, a life and death struggle played itself out on the bloody decks. Howard was cut three times around his throat and neck and received several severe cuts on his arms, face

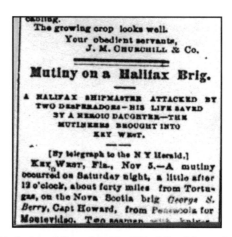

CABLING.
The growing crop looks well.
Your obedient servants,
J. M. CHURCHILL & Co.

## Mutiny on a Halifax Brig.

A HALIFAX SHIPMASTER ATTACKED BY
TWO DESPERADOES – HIS LIFE SAVED
BY A HEROIC DAUGHTER – THE
MUTINEERS BROUGHT INTO
KEY WEST.

[By telegraph to the N Y Herald.]

KEY WEST, Fla., Nov 5.—A mutiny occurred on Saturday night, a little after 12 o'clock, about forty miles from Tortugas, on the Nova Scotia brig *George S. Berry*, Capt Howard, from Pensacola for Montevideo. Two seamen with knives

A *Halifax Herald* clipping of November 10, 1879, tells of the mutiny on the *George S. Berry*.

and back. For fifteen minutes Howard attempted to avoid death, running around and behind various objects on deck.

He found himself near the window of the cabin where his daughter Ida slept and, although he had fallen exhausted to the deck, he called for her to bring up his pistol. She rushed on deck with the gun. One of the mutineers grabbed her by the breast, but Ida quickly pulled up the gun and put it to his head. Britt and Welch lost heart, ran toward the bow of the brig and tried unsuccessfully to get the small boat launched. The mutiny lasted fifteen minutes, but the captain lay near death.

The mate sailed the vessel into the Tortugas where the lightkeepers apprehended the mutineers and lashed them to the rail. *George S. Berry* then sailed to Key West, Florida, where the two men were thrown in jail. Captain Howard received medical attention to the fourteen cuts on his body, the worst of which were to his face. His nose had been cut in two.

Ida gave her statement before the United States Commissioner at Key West: "I am Ida C. Howard, daughter of
Captain Howard. On the night of November 1, after midnight, I was awakened by a scuffle on the starboard side
of the quarter deck near my room. I put on my dress and
heard Papa call, 'Bring me my revolver, Ida!'

"I went on deck and placed it against Welch's head and
said, 'Go, you rascal, or I'll fire.'

"He caught me by my dress, which now shows marks
of blood, and then made a slash around my head with a
knife, but it did not cut. Then I bent down over Papa. Britt
ran forward and Welch followed. I handed Papa the revolver
and ran to the cook's room.

"I called him and came back on deck. I saw four men
standing at the boat, and Papa, standing on deck, said, 'I've
got you now, my bullies,' and he fired.

"When I first came on deck my father had no weapon
and was lying on the deck kicking. He was all bloody.
The deck was so bloody that I slipped in the blood which
splashed up over my feet. The seaman's hand is cut where
the knife slipped through it; also his knee which was cut in
the scuffle."

Ballads and yarns told around the forecastle do not
record the due process of the law or what punishment the
mutineers received for attempting to take over *George S.
Berry*, for attacking Captain Howard and his daughter, and
inflicting knife wounds on both. Reports of the day say Captain Howard recovered from his injuries and that the U.S.
Commissioner reported the case to the Secretary of State
and the Acting British Vice Consul. He, in turn, forwarded
details of the incident to the British Minister stationed in
Washington. As for brave Ida, her name became legend
among tough seadogs of the Atlantic Ocean.

# 20

## The fate of Anglia's oxen

On Monday, September 6, 1880, the Anchor Line screw steamer *Anglia* was on its voyage homeward to London, England, from Boston. It carried general cargo, grain, and about 350 head of cattle, many of which were impounded on deck. The whole cargo was valued at $112,000. In addition to its crew of forty-five, *Anglia* had eleven passengers.

When it reached about sixty miles east of the Grand Banks off Newfoundland, *Anglia* crept along in a dense fog. From out of nowhere the iron barque *Trongate* of Glasgow, deeply laden with railway iron, ploughed into *Anglia* and pierced the ship abaft of the engine room. In the blanket of fog neither ship could see the other.

The second officer of *Anglia* said, "The shock of collision was sudden. The great iron barque of at least one thousand tons was completely veiled from the observations of officers on deck until it swooped down on us like a huge sea bird with outspread wings."

*Trongate* had severe damage, but not of a type to sink the ship. At first, *Anglia*'s officers thought the damage inflicted on their ship was not fatal and it seemed to be within their power to save the steamship. In a way, those misguided thoughts turned out to be the best thing that could have happened.

The idea that *Anglia* could be saved produced cool heads and deliberation among the ship's company. There was no panic among the crew or passengers. The captain calmly ordered all passengers to go into the lifeboats immediately. Following this order, he had the falls and tackles all ready to be used at a moment's notice. Thus the passengers sat in the lifeboats on deck while the crew attempted to keep the steamer afloat.

But the pumps didn't stem the inflow of water and, on examination, officers found eight feet of water in the hold. *Anglia* was rapidly settling down. When it appeared that there was no hope to save the steamer, the captain knew he had to protect the lives of the passengers. A little over an hour had passed since *Trongate* struck *Anglia*. The captain gave the final word to "lower away the lifeboats."

In the meantime, when the barque struck the steamer, many cattle were swept from the deck and into the water. Scores of these were still alive and were milling around in the water near the doomed *Anglia*.

The first lifeboat, filled with twenty crew and passengers and in the charge of the first officer, was lowered and was ready to pull away from the sinking steamer. It was discovered the horns of the oxen, swimming and scrambling for life in the water, had pierced the bottom of the lifeboat. As this lifeboat filled with water, its crew quickly maneuvered it through the milling cattle and back toward the sinking *Anglia*. Another boat – provisioned, watered and supplied with a compass and other necessities – was lowered. In a short time three boats with all *Anglia's* company and passengers moved away from the steamer and headed for the assumed position of the *Trongate.*

As the lifeboats crept through the fog trying to reach a rescue ship which they thought was out there somewhere, but could not see, they were assaulted by cattle. The second officer said, "Our greatest consternation was caused by the frequent assaults of the oxen in their attempts to get on board the boats and the consequent peril of puncturing the sides of the lifeboats. It was only by frequent application of oars and boat hooks that the drowning cattle were stopped from working ruin to the shipwrecked sailors and passengers."

But those in the lifeboats were not sure if *Trongate* was nearby or, if found, in what condition. Many of *Anglia's* company, as they rowed in the dark Atlantic, believed that the blow was so severe that the other ship might not be afloat.

After rowing a half hour, they heard signals from *Tron-gate* and soon were stopped beneath the tall bows of the iron barque. As soon as those aboard the lifeboats were safely on deck, tackles from *Trongate* brought the lifeboats on board as well. A head count determined no one was lost, nor had anyone sustained any injury. There was such a worry and trauma that *Anglia's* three boats were alone in the vast Atlantic with a daunting prospect of trying to reach land that all heaved a sigh of relief and generally congratulated *Trongate's* captain just for being there.

Before *Trongate* steamed away for the nearest port, St. John's, its crew pulled one of the oxen on board. It would provide food, for now the barque had an extra fifty-four people aboard.

FOREIGN CATTLE ON BOARD THE BATAVIER, LONDON AND
ROTTERDAM STEAMER

Cattle and livestock were generally kept in the hold of a ship, but often pens were
constructed on deck, as this image from the *Illustrated London News* of August 26,
1865 shows. When the *Anglia* went down, the cattle below perished; those on deck
were washed overboard.

The New Brunswick newspaper *Saint John Daily Sun*
carried a description of the end of *Anglia* under these headlines:

LOSS OF THE ANGLIA
– Run into by a Bark, Founders at Sea,
An Exciting Scene:

"Hundreds of oxen struggled in the water for hours
around the sides of *Anglia* and *Trongate*. They were left
to their fate and soon followed the sunken *Anglia* to the
bottom. Our boats containing the officers, crew and passengers were not more than a quarter of a mile distant from the
steamer when it sank stern foremost amid the waves.

"This was followed by a terrific detonation, resembling the noise of a dynamite explosion or the thunder of a broadside from a man-o-war. No doubt the boiler exploded, tearing and shattering the steamer into fragments.

"*Anglia*'s officers are unanimous in the opinion that had they remained five minutes longer on the steamer they would have all been swallowed up in the vast maelstrom suction around the sinking steamer."

# 21

## Strange derelicts: The Siddartha and company

In the era of sail and steam one of the most common sources of danger in the ocean was the derelict. Many were partly sunken wrecks of ships that had been abandoned. They lay in wait, inhabiting the most frequented ocean highways and pouncing on unsuspecting wayfarers.

Some hulks remained four or five feet below the surface and were impossible to see even in clear weather, calm seas and with sharp lookouts on the watch. Many a missing ship went down after running into a partially sunken derelict. At one time the governments of the United States and England employed a fleet of vessels to patrol the seas and destroy dangerous wrecks – if they could be found. These countries spent thousands of dollars annually in the hunt for these elusive "ghosts of the sea."

One haunting derelict was the British barque *Cynthia*, found abandoned in August 1881 with all sails set in latitude 48 degrees North, longitude 19 degrees West. A passing ship noticed the strange way *Cynthia* was meandering and upon close inspection it could be seen there was no one on this ship.

Some sailors boarded the derelict. Its hold was nearly full of water and the vessel was in danger of sinking at any moment. Despite the water in the hold, a fire had smouldered in the cargo of cotton. It was assumed sailors had thrown water on the burning cotton. When it became wet, the cargo expanded and forced the seams of *Cynthia* open.

None of *Cynthia's* crew was ever found. But shortly after the discoverers left the ship, it sank. The captain of the American ship *Artropos* of Portland, Maine, described the going down with all sails set as a "mysterious, uncanny sight."

One of the most famous derelicts was the barque *Siddartha*, which had sailed from Jacksonville, Florida, for England on January 26, 1899. Three weeks later in latitude 39 North, longitude 30 West, it met a heavy gale and was wrecked in the storm. On February 22, when the Danish barque *Vernande* came by and picked off the crew, *Siddartha* was abandoned.

This half-sunken ghost of the sea was sighted no less than fifty times by passing ships and was frequently reported to the United States Hydrographic Office in Washington. The last time *Siddartha* was seen it sailed unattended off the coast of Ireland, where it was taken into tow by a British steamer.

Equally dangerous was the Norwegian barque *Taurus*, sighted eighteen times before it was destroyed. *Taurus*, wrecked in a storm while on a voyage from Ship Island, Mississippi, to France, lay for many months in the direct path of transatlantic traffic. Two ships struck this derelict, but without

THE WATER-LOGGED SHIP JANE LOWDEN –

FROM A SKETCH BY A PASSENGER ON BOARD THE GRESHAM

The derelict *Jane Lowden*, twenty-eight days waterlogged and in a sinking condition, was abandoned Feburary 1866 en route from Quebec to England. The crew of seventeen, except Captain Casey, perished – some by drowning, some by hunger or thirst. Eight went to the maintop when the hull sank under water. In the picture from the *Illustrated London News*, February 17, 1866, the *Gresham* approachs the *Jane Lowden*.

fatal damage. Finally, after numerous complaints from steamer captains, it was destroyed.

Shipping authorities noticed and documented that derelicts congregated at certain points along the Atlantic seaboard and followed more or less definite courses in their wanderings. If a ship was abandoned in mid-Atlantic it somehow drifted back to the American or Canadian coast. Over the years many were plotted off Sable Island. In a review of certain ghosts of the sea, the newspaper *Trade Review* (July 1901) said, "There are more than 100 derelicts half sunken or barely moving off Sable Island." Wrecks often assembled around Cape Cod as well.

The tale of the renowned ship *Marie Celeste* (often mistakenly called *Mary Celeste*) bears summarizing here. *Marie Celeste* was launched at Spencer's Island, Nova Scotia, near the head of the Bay of Fundy under the name *Amazon*. Following an accidental grounding at Cow Bay, Cape Breton, in 1868, the vessel was repaired, renamed, and sold to American interests.

On December 5, 1872, it was found drifting in relatively good order by the vessel *Del Gratia* off Gibraltar. *Del Gratia*'s crew saw a ship which seemed to be sailing without the aid of a crew. Captain Moorhouse sent a three-man boarding party to investigate. The sailors found no one aboard and, although slightly battered by the weather, *Marie Celeste* was deemed seaworthy. Everything was left just as if the crew was still aboard, but no one ever satisfactorily explained what had happened to Captain Briggs, his wife, infant child and crew of seven.

There are other cases as strange as *Marie Celeste*. Nine years after the *Marie Celeste* story broke, the *Ellen Austin* encountered a schooner – with no crew and little cargo – in the Atlantic. Men from *Ellen Austin* boarded the abandoned ship to take it as a prize. Then a storm separated the vessels. When *Ellen Austin* made contact again, the boarding crew had disappeared. The lure of a big salvage reward drew a second crew to the drifting schooner. They put up a little sail and soon the ghostly derelict was sailing further and further ahead of *Ellen Austin*. The speeding schooner vanished over the horizon forever – two boarding crews and the mysterious derelict disappeared without a trace.

According to the United States Hydrographic Office in a bulletin issued in 1921, an average of eight vessels a year were wrecked or damaged in the North Atlantic by collision

THE BOSTON GLOBE—WEDNESDAY, NOVEMBER 3, 1920

## ABANDONED VESSEL FOUND PLOWING SEAS

### Nordica Picked Up Right in Steamship Track

### Damage to Rudder Only Apparent

### Trouble—Towed to Boston

After sailing hundreds of miles without a hand at the helm the British fishing schooner Nordica was towed into the lower harbor early yesterday by the

The *Marie Celeste* was just one of many mysteriously abandoned ships in the era of sail. *The Boston Globe* likens the drifting *Nordica* to the *Marie Celeste* – afloat for days in good condition and with no one aboard.

with derelicts. By the mid-1920s the office estimated no less than thirty derelicts drifted somewhere in the ocean.

Satisfactory explanations for how and why certain ships became abandoned hulks were told every now and then. One prime example was the *Marion G. Douglas*, which made Nova Scotian marine history when it was found drifting and abandoned but practically intact on November 28, 1919, off the Scilly Islands of Cornwall, in the British Isles.

Scilly Islanders of Brighter Island, who happened upon the abandoned schooner, found the derelict had a cargo of wood in its hold; thus there was no danger of the mysterious ship sinking quickly. Its name was clearly visible on the stern: *Marion G. Douglas*. Lloyd's Registry of Shipping revealed it was built at Fox River, Nova Scotia, in 1917 and was registered to W.N. Reinhardt of LaHave.

When Captain Sydney Corkum and his crew arrived in Halifax on December 2, they explained how, in a fierce Atlantic storm, they were forced to abandon *Marion G. Douglas* on November 14. They were picked up by the S.S. *Suffolk* and brought to Halifax.

Salvors and crew revealed the circumstances by which the two-masted schooner *Nordica* became a derelict. Owned in Grand Bank, Newfoundland, *Nordica*, with sails set and in sound condition, was found drifting and abandoned in mid-Atlantic in 1921. The abandoned ship was towed to Boston where salvors determined that *Nordica* had a damaged steering apparatus. Its crew, thinking the schooner was unmanageable in the gale, climbed into a lifeboat and rowed away from their vessel. They were later picked up by the liner *Wilfaro* bound for New York.

When the crew arrived back home in Grand Bank, they had to explain how they had left the sinking *Nordica* in mid-ocean. Much to the embarrassment of the crew, a few days later the news came from Boston that the *Nordica* was there, in good condition. Patten and Forsey's of Grand Bank paid the salvage claim and reacquired their schooner.

# 22

## *Missing, presumed lost*

Despite the tales of ships abandoned, schooners struck by steamers, others sinking and drifting, or lost on rocky coasts, there were other vessels that became casualties of a more mundane foe: wind and wave. Some of these ships, left alone to face tremendous gales on a vast ocean, were simply overwhelmed by tremendous odds and vanished from sight.

The August and September Gales, the diminishing winds or the "tail end" of tropical hurricanes was a weather phenomenon much respected by early fishing bank captains. Their sixty- to one-hundred-ton schooners were often caught without warning far from land, often with disastrous results. In an earlier era there were no five-day weather forecasts and the gales were likely to pounce suddenly, often within an hour or two, giving no time to sail to safe anchorage.

In the late summer of 1883 two ships disappeared within a month of each other – one loss was attributed to an August Gale. The schooner *James Bliss* sailed for the fishing banks from Gloucester in August. This 62-ton banker, built in Essex, Massachusetts, in 1868, carried twelve fishermen.

It had not been heard from since the Gale of August 26. Owners stated the schooner was well-provisioned and seaworthy in all respects. Owners William Parsons and Company said the *James Bliss* had 106 hogsheads of salt aboard but, according to local newspapers of November 2, 1883, the fact that the schooner had not reported into any port for bait and water for nearly ten weeks "renders the prospect of it returning to any port very dark indeed." During all this time there were large numbers of vessels constantly on the fishing grounds and most had taken good catches. If *James Bliss* were still afloat, it should have been seen by some of the fishing fleet.

The October issue of Nova Scotia's *Liverpool Times* voiced the opinion that all hopes of the safety of *James Bliss* were given up. For Liverpool, on the southeastern tip of Nova Scotia, this statement was traumatic. Most of the men on *James Bliss* were from seaside villages approximately eighty miles from Liverpool: Captain Rupert D. Jeffery and Henry Smith were from Argyle; Joseph Surrette, Henry Surrette, Louis Babine, Peter White, Ambrose White, Louis Doucette, and Edward Muise hailed from Eel Brook.

The November 2, 1883, *Cape Ann Advertiser*, under its banner "Missing Vessel Given Up," said, "It is our sad duty to publish the intelligence of the probable loss of two more vessels of the fishing fleet with all on board. Days and weeks have passed and it was hoped by those having relatives and friends on board that they would someday witness these missing vessels proudly sailing up the harbour. But time has passed and not a word of hope, not a gleam of information relative to the vessels has been received . . ."

The second vessel missing was Gloucester's *Charles H. Hildreth*. It had gone to George's Bank on September 17 and seven weeks had gone by without a word of its whereabouts. It had not been sighted nor heard from since it left. There was no violent gale during that period; it can only be assumed it had been run down during the night by some steamer and sent to the bottom with all crew. Wonson Brothers owned the 58-ton vessel built in Gloucester in 1867, and had insured it for $3,460 with the Gloucester Mutual Fishing Insurance Company.

As publicized in local newspapers, the names of the ten men aboard the *Charles H. Hildreth* were not entirely accurate. Captain Michael McGinley, John G. Marston, Patrick Sullivan, John Thebedore, John B. Brown, Antoine Hismond and Charles Monroe had fished on various Gloucester vessels for years and were most likely on the missing schooner. The remaining three were thought to have been newly hired crew and probably from Nova Scotia.

Perhaps today it would unthinkable for a ship to leave port without clear and accurate names and addresses of its crew. But the lack of information on a crew from the era of sail only adds to the mystery of a vanished ship.

# 23

## Steamship horror

*April 1884*

Captain Schoonhoven said he, his crew and passengers had a pleasant voyage all the way across the Atlantic from Antwerp to Halifax. "We had," he stated in his official report, "13½ days with nothing particular to report. Then on the evening of April 3 [1884] we had dense fog, heavy rains, brilliant lightning. At 6 p.m. I saw what I thought was Chebucto Head light about 25 miles ahead. About 10 or 20 minutes later I discovered it was the fixed light off Sambro at the approaches to Halifax harbour."

His ship was the S.S. *Daniel Steinmann*, an iron ship of 1,785 tons owned by Steinmann and Ludwig of Antwerp, Belgium. On its final voyage it had ninety passengers and a crew of thirty-five men. Of the passengers, fourteen (two families) were ticketed to Sherbrooke, Quebec, where they intended to settle; the others were bound for New York. The steamer also had a general cargo of 350 tons destined for Halifax.

In error the great steamer now found itself near the Mad Rock Shoal, about three hundred yards south of the Sambro lighthouse. By the time the officers of the S.S. *Daniel Steinmann* realized their perilous position, it was too late. Soundings told the captain there were only twenty-six fathoms (156 feet) under the ship.

"I ordered the helm hard aport," said Schoonhoven. "But a minute afterwards, the steamer struck heavily but drifted over the ledge. The anchors were let down. Then the crew and passengers came running on deck and I ordered the first and second officers to launch the boats and get the women and children into them. All this time the vessel continued to drift and drag her anchors, getting nearer and nearer to the breakers, which were quite visible, the sea breaking over the ship in immense waves."

*Daniel Steinmann* struck lightly at first. The next time it hit Mad Rock Shoal, the vessel lost its rudder and broke its propeller. The third time, the ship bumped heavily amidships and knocked a large hole in its bottom.

At least an hour and a half (another survivor estimated about twenty minutes) elapsed from the time *Daniel Steinmann* first struck until it sank. During that time the most unimaginable confusion and consternation erupted on the ship. According to reports, it was a time of "Every man for himself and the devil take the hindmost."

Three of the four lifeboats went down with the ship. The fourth was cut away by a seaman and seven men were rescued in it. There was no discernible effort to save the women and children. The captain stated: "All this time I was on the bridge, but I now ran forward to ascertain if the cable had parted, and had just reached the foremast when the ship again struck. At the same time an immense wave came pouring over her, carrying off every living soul. There was one despairing wail from strong men, weak women and innocent children. The wail arose above the fury and tumult of the waves, and then the ship settled down into the waves with the rapidity of lightning.

"It was so quick I was obliged to let go the rigging, up which I was climbing, and rise with the water. On coming to the surface I found myself beside the yardarm which was only about two feet above the surface of the water. I clutched the ropes and succeeded in dragging myself on to it. I had not been long seated before somebody came floating by. I clutched him and drew him on to the yard. He proved to be a passenger, a young man named Saco Nikolo, bound for New York.

"We prepared to swim to shore, but the masts stood secure, and we remained in our perilous position for seven hours, until rescued by a Mr. Gilkie who came for us in one of our own boats. Up to that time I was not aware that anybody except myself and Nikolo had been saved."

One hundred and twenty-four crew and passengers perished, of which only a few bodies were recovered. Captain Schoonhoven, the passenger, and seven crewmen of *Daniel Steinmann* survived. One other officer, second bosun Fritz Nich, survived. In some respects his statement to the court of inquiry agrees with the captain: "I was at the port bow, helping to get [a lifeboat] out. All the crew had been called up after the ship struck the first time and were on deck and, with the passengers, were at or near the boats.

"As soon as I left the anchor I rushed back to the lifeboat and got in at the stern, cutting it adrift. Just at that moment a heavy wave swept over the ship, under which it sank. A number of people jumped into the boat at the same moment. The ropes at the bow had been cut, but not those at the stern. The result was that the lifeboat went down bow first with the ship and, as it went down, I sprang out of the stern and into the jolly boat. I don't know anything about the boats on the starboard side.

"When I called the first mate I noticed that he put on his gold watch and a big ring on his finger. These were presented to him at his marriage six months ago. When his body was found ashore on the island by the fishermen they were both missing.

"I was saved in the jolly boat and landed on the island. There was great excitement on the ship after she struck; the passengers and crew alike were shouting, swearing and praying. In the confusion that prevailed, it is impossible for me to even form an idea of the time that elapsed between when the ship first struck and when she sank. I regard Captain Schoonhoven as a capable and thorough seaman."

The loss of so many lives at the approaches to Halifax had shipping agencies researching and enumerating the many shipwrecks along the Nova Scotian coast. Almost exactly eleven years previously, the White Star liner *Atlantic* went ashore at Meagher's Island, near Prospect, about five miles west of where *Daniel Steinmann* went down.

---

*Notable shipwrecks along the Nova Scotia coast between 1873 and 1884:*

*Atlantic*, Meagher's Island
*City of Washington*, Little Port L'Herbet, Shelburne County
*Valetta*, near Lockeport
*Boston City*, Mud Island
*Moravian*, Mud Island
*Cedar Grove*, Tor Bay, Guysborough
*Scud*, Lunenburg
*Dacian*, Jeddore
*State of Virginia*, Sable Island
*Daniel Steinmann*, Halifax

---

# 24

## An odd twist of fate at Cape Race

*July 1884*

$\mathcal{M}$any areas of the North American coastline from Cape Hatteras to the northern reaches of Newfoundland have been given the dubious honour of being named "a dangerous coast" because of the large number of ship losses through the centuries. Leading the way would be Sable Island, the Cape Cod promontory and Cape Race.

Certainly Cape Race and vicinity deserves the terms treacherous, dangerous, a graveyard and other equally disreputable names. Official accounts, folklore and anecdotes continuously refer to strong currents, tides, fog, remoteness and rugged landscape in the Cape Race neighbourhood which have lured many a good ship to its doom.

WRECK OF THE SWEDISH SLOOP-OF-WAR ORADD, NEAR RYE.

*Harrington's* shipwrecked crew were able to reach a beach at Cape Race, Newfoundland. In this similar situation, the Swedish sloop *Oradd* is aground in southeast England. (*Illustrated London News*, December 15, 1866)

One of the best illustrations of tidal power combined with a wild and rugged shore is the tale of the wreck of the English steamer *Hartington* in 1884. The vessel had sailed halfway around the world and back when it was lost at St. Shotts, near Cape Race.

The steamer left West Hartlepool, England, in March 1884 for Port Said, Gulf of Aden. Departing Port Said, it entered the Mediterranean, traveling to Messenia in Greece, and Palermo in Sicily. From the Mediterranean it steamed across the Atlantic to South Carolina, thence to Sydney, Cape Breton, to take a cargo of rock phosphates to Dublin, Ireland.

With such an itinerary S.S. *Hartington* is reminiscent of the British "tramp" steamers that plied the oceans of the world, made famous in fiction by writers like Robert Louis Stevenson, Joseph Conrad and Rudyard Kipling. But on the occasion the steamer attempted to pass Cape Race, its days were numbered.

*Hartington* refueled with coal at Sydney and left on July 11, 1884. Its compass had been tested and tried true and its course charted for east-southeast. It would have passed Cape Race by at least thirty miles. The weather was thick and continued hazy until midday on the 12th when the steamer had run about 153 miles by dead reckoning.

When conditions became foggy, the crew could not see a ship's length ahead. At midnight the captain took soundings and figured he was crossing the edge of Green Bank, about fifty miles southwest of Cape Race. Soundings showed about seventy fathoms (420 feet). Since the captain believed he was on course he did not order more soundings.

As an extra precaution because of the fog, the ship ran at half speed from midday July 12 through Sunday, the 13th. At 5:30 a.m. Sunday it went ashore near St. Shotts, a little west of Cape Race. The captain said later that strong currents pulling the ship northerly was the reason it was off course.

The crew had no warning. Breakers loomed up in the fog and darkness a couple of minutes before the steamer ground ashore. Although the engines were put at full astern there was no time to save the ship. The fore compartments filled with water at once and the crew knew immediately the ship would sink. Thus the engines were stopped before they pulled *Hartington* off the jagged ledge and into deeper water.

In a twist of fate, the fog lifted within minutes after the steamer went ashore on the reef – too late to save *Hartington* but time enough to save another steamer in its company. The S.S. *Foscolia*, having left Sydney just behind *Hartington*, was a short distance astern. Both were close together coming along the south coast of Newfoundland. *Foscolia* would have shared the same fate had not the fog lifted shortly after the *Hartington* went aground. *Foscolia* too was in the grip of a strong inset of tide that apparently took both steamers off course.

On board *Foscolia* the men on the bridge saw the breakers and the wreck of *Hartington* and swung away in time to avoid the treacherous reefs.

Immediately after stranding, *Hartington's* captain and other seamen set out in the steamer's small boat for the nearest inhabited place. Due to the drift of objects that had been thrown overboard, the captain realized the tide was very strong landward, perhaps running at about five or six knots. The tide was so strong that the same small boat, when it made an attempt to get back to *Hartington*, could not stem the current although manned by four able seamen. It had to go back to the beach.

In fact, *Hartington's* captain learned from the fishermen at St. Shotts and vicinity that since the preceding Thursday, July 10, when there had been a heavy wind from the south, the current was running as fast as eight knots.

As for the fate of the S.S. *Hartington*, a Marine Court of Inquiry held in St. John's determined the captain and crew of the steamer were not to blame. The inset of tide at Cape Race and St. Shotts made the wreck "An Act of God."

# 25

## A night on a rock

When the ordeal was over and the surviving crew were safe ashore at Gloucester, Massachusetts, it was the two Newfoundland fishermen who told the story. Joseph Holland and Nicholas Ryan were part of a crew of fourteen on the *Twilight*, owned by a Nova Scotian business, which left Canso on July 21 for the Grand Banks.

Captain Lemuel Hines had done well by early September, salting down a thousand quintals (about 112,000 pounds) of cod. He was making for home on September 11 about 9:30 p.m. The wind was southerly, the seas rough. Hines believed he was nearing Cranberry Island light, but probably erred in navigation with the wind and current.

The *Twilight* struck on Shag Rock, a sunken reef off what was called the White Pine – one of the most dangerous localities off Nova Scotia. Holland recalled, "As soon as the

## Wreck of the Royal Mail Company's steamship Rhone off St. Peter's Island, West Indies

When a ship like the *Twilight* sank near land, a lucky crew may be able to escape to a rock. In this representative sketch, the steamship *Rhone*, although near the shore, was lost with all crew and passengers. (*Illustrated London News*, December 14, 1867)

vessel struck, the starboard dory was hoisted out and immediately entered by Captain Hines, William Berrigan and another crewman with a Frenchman, whose name I cannot recall right now. The first sea that struck after the *Twilight* was on the rock swept all the dories off the deck, and we were left without any means of escape.

"The same sea that carried away the other dories struck the captain's dory. A loose chain swung out from the wreck, killing Captain Hines and Berrigan instantly. The Frenchman was not seen after and probably drowned."

In an instant everything was swept from the decks and the remaining crew had to jump for a rock. Two came close to not making it, the captain's young nephew Stanwood Hines and another fisherman. Nicholas Ryan picked up the story: "It was too far for these two to jump and there was little room on the islet. The boy was in the water for nearly a half hour and I finally got to him and pulled him on the rock. We rolled and rolled him to get the water out of him, even though I was badly bruised all over my body. We also got to Eldridge Larkin, who was in the water one and a half hours.

"Shag Rock was not large enough to hold eleven men. There was nothing left of the wreck, certainly not enough for anyone to cling to. Holland tried to swim out to the wreck and get something so we could have something to hold us on the rock, but it was no use. Holland lost his oil jacket in the attempt.

"There we were on a little rock, the waves breaking high and threatening to engulf the eleven of us who had succeeded in reaching the spot. We were huddled together in one heap, minus hats and some without boots and coats. The tide was rising fast and some of the men were slipping off the rock and being helped back again. One fellow did not seem to care whether he stayed on the rock or not."

Weakened by the pounding they took when *Twilight* grounded, the bruises suffered in the jump to Shag Rock and the dashing of the waves over their refuge, some of the crew were exhausted. One man found a section of plank three inches wide and about three feet long, the only piece of debris from the schooner. This was placed in a crevice and Nicholas Ryan sat down to hold one side while opposite him, holding up the slender stake, was another crewman. They sat that way for four hours, the rest of the men hanging on to those holding the stake. The sea rose higher and dashed over Shag Rock.

Ryan said, "We thought that even if a small boat got out to us, it would be impossible for it to live [get near the rock]. Every man thought his time had come."

Eventually the tide receded, seas calmed somewhat and, with the morning breaking, the eleven castaways were in better circumstances. As soon as the sun rose, they saw two men on Cranberry Island. It was the lighthouse keeper and his assistant. Much to the chagrin of the disheartened men on the rock, they made no attempt to row to the Shag Rock, but pulled away seemingly toward Canso.

At 10:30 a.m., the schooner *George E. Harrold* and Captain Rial Lyons discovered the shipwrecked mariners, took them off and carried them into Canso. After surviving for thirteen hours on an exposed rock, the eleven shipwrecked sailors told rescuers they could not have lasted another hour. In their weakened condition, the rising tide would have washed them off the crag.

Ryan remarked that he felt rather lame from being bruised by the rocks and his hands and body were scarred. Berrigan's remains were found four days after the wreck, Captain Hines' a week after. Hines, age twenty-eight, left a wife and one child.

The two men who related the story, Newfoundlanders Holland and Ryan (although their actual place of residence is not given), were carried to Gloucester in the Greenland vessel *Mist*.

As for the people of Canso, they were astonished to hear that eleven had lived upon Shag Rock for all those hours. The bird hunters of the area said that spray dashes over the crag even when the tide is low and the weather calm.

# 26

## Collision at sea

July 1886

There are many documented and reported collisions at sea. Newspapers found the tales made good copy, especially when one or both ships went down or there was loss of life. As well, marine court reports were publicized, for the law of the sea dictates an investigation or marine enquiry be held when ships collide. However, many schooners were run down and the personnel on the larger ship weren't even aware of an accident. If anyone on the smaller ship survived the collision they told of the horror. Regrettably, there were other steamer captains who, knowing they had struck something, journeyed on without doubling back to see what had happened.

Relatives of sailors "lost without a trace" swear their loved ones' ships were cut down and the accident never reported. Of course, there is the possibility that the larger ship was aware of a collision, but by the time it stopped or turned around, the smaller ship was gone to the bottom, taking its crew with it.

There is an unofficial tale from a passenger on the transatlantic liner *City of Paris* who said that one night as the steamer was crossing the Grand Banks in a storm, watchmen on the bridge noticed something odd on the forecastle head. On close examination, it was discovered to be ten feet of a schooner's mast lying on the deck. This was reported to the captain, who presumed that in the storm they had cut down a fishing boat – probably at anchor – and part of its mast had fallen on deck. Not one person had the slightest knowledge of, or had heard any noise to signal, such a tragedy. The fate of the unfortunate schooner's crew can only be imagined.

The French fishing schooner *Sybille* left St. Malo on March 11, 1886, with a crew of seventeen hands and fully equipped for the season's fishing off Newfoundland. By July 20 the vessel had done well and had nearly a full load of cod aboard. That day the weather could only be described as a thick fog, a virtual shroud of grey.

At 10:30 p.m. *Sybille* was at anchor and the crew had the proper "at anchor" lights burning. As was the regulation for fishing vessels working on the Banks and in proximity with the European-American shipping routes, the ship's bell was rung at set intervals. In other words, the crew did everything possible to help their vessel avoid a collision with a steamer.

But then the crew heard the whistle of a steamer somewhere to the westward. As they later learned, this was the S.S. *Nova Scotian*, a screw steamship of 3,300 tons carrying eighty-four crewmen on a voyage from Halifax, Nova Scotia, to Newfoundland.

*Sybille*'s bell continued ringing and its master blew the fog horn. Shortly afterwards those on board *Sybille* could hear water rushing from the bows of the steamer and then saw the three lights, followed by an iron hull looming up in the fog. *Nova Scotian* was fifty to a hundred yards off, a little before the beam on the starboard side of the French vessel, heading straight for the smaller craft. It was obvious no one on *Nova Scotian* heard or saw anything, nor were they concerned about reducing speed in the thick fog.

Despite all precautions, the stem of *Nova Scotian* struck the starboard midships of *Sybille*, cutting almost through it and doing so much damage the vessel sank in a few minutes. Except for one man who drowned in trying to get off the schooner, all on board survived without injury or mishap.

In March 1887, court proceedings began to determine where the blame lay. According to statements from the defense lawyers for *Nova Scotian*, just before the collision the ship was making about eight to nine knots with the engines going half speed and its steam whistle sounding at regular intervals.

Under these assumed safeguards and conditions, those on the bridge of the steamer heard a single blast of a fog horn from another vessel and they stopped the engines at once. A minute or so after, *Nova Scotian*'s crew saw a small white light about two hundred feet distant. They claimed there was no anchor light visible in the schooner's rigging.

The engines of the steamer were put full speed astern and the helm turned hard a-starboard. Thereupon, a loud shouting and a bell could be heard from *Sybille*. The *Nova Scotian*'s stem and bowsprit collided with the starboard side of *Sybille* between the fore and mainmast. *Sybille* quickly sank.

Mr. C. Hall and Dr. Stubbs appeared for the plaintiffs, the captain and owner of *Sybille*. It was proven that *Sybille* did indeed have all its lights burning, including the anchor light high in the rigging. It was the correct kind of light and properly hung. The captain and officers on the bridge of the steamer could not or did not see the light. It was further proven *Sybille* sounded its fog signals at proper intervals in accordance with the international rules for vessels at anchor in a fog.

**COLLISION CASE.**

**THE STEAMER "NOVA SCOTIAN" TO BLAME FOR RUNNING DOWN A FRENCH FISHING VESSEL.**

(*From the Halifax Herald.*)

This was an action of collision. According to the statement of claim, the "Sybille,"

The judge's ruling was against the steamer, as reported by the *Halifax Herald* in late March 1887.

In his summation, Mr. Justice Butt ruled the steamer was going at an excessive speed in thick fog and over an area frequented by fishing vessels. He said, "I am perfectly aware of what the exigencies of commerce demand and of the need to carry passengers as rapidly as possible, but I do not think all those considerations together justify running through a number of fishing vessels in a fog at nine knots an hour. I, therefore, hold that the *Nova Scotian* was alone to blame for the collision."

# 27

## The loss of the Charles Graham

January 1887

*W*hen the news came through there were survivors from the schooner *Charles Graham*, the local paper put its headline in bold: **SAVED Miraculous Escape from a Watery Grave.** On February 1, 1887, news reached Halifax, Nova Scotia, that the crew of the schooner *Charles Graham* "before reported lost with all hands near Prospect, had been saved."

The report was only partly correct – five of the schooner's six crew had escaped death; the sixth, the captain, had drowned. The account of the tragedy was given to Charles H. Harvey, who in turn sent it to James Morash, the justice of the peace at West Dover.

A sworn statement, dated January 26, 1887, came from *Charles Graham*'s mate, James A. Watt: "On the evening of January 9, 1887, we left St. George's, Bermuda. The weather was contrary to our passage. We proceeded on our way bound for Halifax. We made Cape Sable light on the evening of January 23 and on Monday, the 24th, we made at or near Peggy's Point, but did not see the light.

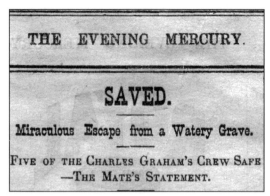

Headline from the St. John's *Evening Mercury*, February 1, 1887.

"We wore ship [sailed away] and stood westward for about two hours under double reefs. We could not see land. We then . . . headed south by east.

"About 8 o'clock in the evening we thought all was right. About 10 o'clock our vessel struck on an unknown rock. I cut the foremast away, which lodged on a cliff, to which myself and four of the crew escaped.

"The island cliff proved to be Dover Castle, an island rock at the south entrance of Dover harbour. The captain did not try to save himself as far as I know. We remained on the rock until Wednesday, the 26th, when we were taken off by the inhabitants of Dover and kindly cared for.

"The vessel is a total wreck. Cargo likely lies near the scene of the disaster. I could not say if sails and rigging will be saved."

After his rescue from the wreck, Mate Watt lived with a Mr. Smeltzer on Dover Island. By January 28, he arrived in Halifax where he resided. His wife, who had heard the first reports there were no survivors, received the news her husband and four others – Anthony Boudrot, Angus Morrigo, James Crotty and the African-Canadian cook George Thompson – survived. *Charles Graham's* captain was John Coleridge, who resided in Halifax but was born in Newfoundland.

# 28

## Fifty-six hours in the rigging

*May 1888*

It was 5 o'clock in the morning, May 23, 1888. The *Larnica* steamed along in the North Atlantic, approximate longitude 41 West, latitude 42 North. According to the newspaper *Brooklyn Eagle*, *Larnica* was owned in Windsor, Nova Scotia, and Captain M. Boyd of Philadelphia was in command with his brother Joseph as first mate. As dawn broke, Joseph Boyd alerted the captain to a strange sight in the ocean.

"It looked like a wreck, an abandoned vessel about ten miles from us," said mate Boyd. "As we had to pass that way, we ran down to see if there were any people on board." As *Larnica* drew closer, Boyd said, he saw a ragged shirt flying from a portion of the only mast left standing.

*Larnica's* crew could see signs of life on the wreck – several people were tied to the rigging. Hammocks made of old sails were lashed across the rigging, behind which the captain,

WRECK OF THE AFRICAN MAIL STEAMSHIP ARMENIAN ON THE
ARKLOW BANK, ST. GEORGE'S CHANNEL

After fifty-six hours tied to the rigging, most of the crew of *Zouave* survived. In this picture, when the ship *Armenian* sank in the Irish Sea in 1865, eight lives were lost. Some crewmen, still gripping mainmast lines and ropes, were found alive by the steamer *Montegue*. (*Illustrated London News*, February 4, 1865)

officers and a portion of the crew were crouched. This was their only protection from the high seas breaking over the decks.

Joseph Boyd continued, "We hove our ship to and with difficulty launched a lifeboat. Five men proceeded to the wreck at the risk of losing their own lives. It was a dangerous undertaking, but the crew made up their minds to reach the disabled vessel or die in the attempt. To keep the lifeboat afloat in such a heavy sea was no easy matter, but our boys reached there and took off the captain who was sick and half the crew. These were brought safely to our ship."

The determined lifeboat crew from *Larnica* were bosun John Potter (the son of the late Captain Potter of St. John's, Newfoundland), second mate Smith, and three other seamen. Once the first group of shipwrecked mariners were aboard the rescue ship, Captain Boyd learned the vessel was the American ship *Zouave*, out of Boston and commanded by Captain Soper. It had a cargo of pitch pine timber.

While the captain talked to the first group of sailors, rescuers were making a second trip back to the sea-wracked hulk. From his position on the side of *Larnica*, Boyd watched the little boat cautiously work its way back to the derelict and recalled, "I thought at times the lifeboat would be swamped and all hands lost. Eventually, they got to the wreck and took off all the crew remaining. We treated them as well as we could and brought them to Brooklyn [New York]."

Captain Soper immediately went home to Boston and the rest of the crew found accommodations in the Sailors' Home in New York. When the reporter from *Brooklyn Eagle* wanted details about *Zoauve*, first mate A. Richmond described how his vessel was wrecked: "The *Zouave* left Mobile [Alabama] April 20. In the gale of wind that lasted from May 17 to the 20th, the ship capsized, but it righted itself again.

"When the ship turned over, the cook, who was in the cabin attending to his duties, was killed by the wreckage. As well a seaman, known only by his nickname as Scotch, was washed overboard, never to be seen again.

"We were fifty-six hours in the rigging, waiting for death. In any form at that time, death would have been a welcome guest, for we were without food or water during those hours. But the good ship *Larnica* came into sight and rescued us just when hope had almost fled.

"The wreck cannot founder or sink until it rots, for the cargo is timber and that will keep it afloat for many a day."

*Zouave*, Richmond said, had a crew of fifteen and all, except the two who died during the storm, were brought to Brooklyn safely. When abandoned, *Zouave* was drifting southward and out of the track of all European steamers.

As the story of the timely rescue circulated around Brooklyn, a great number of people went to the foot of Richards Street, looking at and admiring the *Larnica*, which had saved the lives of so many sailors. Second mate Smith and bosun Potter of *Larnica* received medals from the Boston Humane Society. Captain Soper was presented with a gold watch from the American government.

# 29

## *Fulda: Guilty or not?*

*July 1888*

On July 18, 1888, the steamship *Fulda* pulled into New York and reported it had run down an unknown fishing schooner on the Banks of Newfoundland four days previously. It was foggy at the time and the schooner disappeared astern almost immediately after the collision. Commanded by Captain Ringk, *Fulda* was a passenger ship of the North German Lloyd line and had left Bremen for New York.

Moments after *Fulda* struck, the entire crew of the hapless schooner, about twenty men, were on deck, clinging to the rigging and shouting for help. The wrecked vessel was a large two-masted banking schooner and carried about sixteen dories. The air was filled with terrified and frantic shouts, which prompted all the passengers of *Fulda* to leave the breakfast table and rush to the deck.

According to the officers of *Fulda*, the fishermen, who wore red shirts and red caps, shouted loudly, "Ave Maria." Some of them tried to climb up the side of the steamer, but slipped back into the water before assistance could be given.

It wasn't clear if the whole crew of fishermen perished, as several of *Fulda*'s passengers had thrown a number of life preservers overboard. As soon as the steamer was brought to a standstill, it was turned around and for over an hour crew searched for the wreck or its victims. There was no trace of either.

In a statement issued later by Captain Ringk, he said he believed *Fulda* had only struck the schooner's bowsprit and had sheared it off. It was completely unnecessary for the passengers, who he claimed had become overly excited, to toss life preservers over the side. He blamed the neglectful fishermen who did not sound the vessel's bells in foggy conditions.

# 30

## *A most remarkable escape*

In the era of sail, the volume of sea traffic off the treacherous sands of Cape Cod and Massachusetts Bay was so great that several lifeguard stations were set up along the coast. Each station was equipped with longboats, wheeled cannon for launching ropes, breeches buoys, and teams of lifeguards who patrolled the coast looking for ships in distress. One station was established at Scituate, Massachusetts, located about twenty miles southwest of Boston.

The station at Scituate became the scene of a most unusual wreck during a storm of November 26, 1888. All evening the wind raged. Shortly after midnight patrolmen discovered a wrecked vessel in the mountainous seas at the southern entrance of the harbour. There was no sign of life on or near the vessel. In the high surf and winds there was no way to get to the stranded craft.

THE RICHARD LEWIS LIFE-BOAT LANDING A SHIPWRECKED CREW
AT PENZANCE

A pen and ink rendering of a lifeboat landing a shipwrecked crew off the *John Gray* at Penzance, England. Six refused to take the perilous trip in the lifeboat and later drowned. (*Illustrated London News*, January 26, 1867)

The vessel was badly broken up, and wreckage was strewn all along the shore and inside Scituate harbour. Those who examined the debris saw the dories, fishing tubs and haddock and knew the unfortunate craft was a fishing vessel. One body was picked up by the lifestation crew and it was hoped it could be identified by friends or relatives. He was about thirty-five years old, five feet eight inches in height, and weighed about 175 to 180 pounds. All that day, November 27, the crew of the station scoured the shore searching for items with the vessel's name and for more bodies of the ill-fated crew, for all believed there could be no survivors.

That day news came from Boston that the wrecked vessel was the *Norton*, owned by Stubbs of Boston's famed T Wharf. At first it was thought all fifteen aboard had perished, but the story of a survivor emerged, a man named Allan. In the St, John's, Newfoundland, *Evening Mercury* of December 28, 1888, his tale appeared under the headline A Man Named Allan Had a Most Remarkable Escape: ". . . [Fog] was so thick that it was impossible to see 100 yards, and the vessel was not discovered till nearly midnight. At daylight a survivor was seen to crawl out from under its hull. He was very weak from exposure and could give but little information. He said the vessel came in by Peaked Hill Bars on Sunday morning and steered northwest for Boston, against the wishes of the crew who proposed to put into Provincetown.

"It was a terrible day. As near as Allan could tell they struck between 5 and 6 Sunday afternoon and almost immediately capsized. He was down below and was the only one saved. He says the *Norton* carried fifteen men and one deck boy.

"After the wreck was discovered, Allan was still in the hull and nearly drowned. He could barely keep his head out of water, but could plainly hear the voices of those on the beach, and had to wait hours till the sea left the ship. He barely had strength enough to crawl out. He was much exhausted and was taken to the residence of John Conroy and kindly cared for."

# 31

## An extraordinary tale of survival

On August 15 the *Hope* sailed from Nash's Creek, New Brunswick. One month later, on September 16, the schooner *Amelia C.* brought three men, *Hope*'s sole survivors, back to Halifax. The barque was probably floating bottom up in the ocean; six men had gone down with their ship.

*Hope*, a 276-ton vessel, was built in Quebec in 1865 and owned in Aberystwyth, Wales. Most of the crew, including Captain David Jenkins, were from Aberystwyth. On August 15, 1892, it sailed from Nash's Creek laden with deals, or large squared pieces of timber, destined for that renowned shipbuilding centre, Port Madoc (Porthmadog), Wales.

In addition to a full load in the holds, *Hope* had a large deck load of timber. A week later, while forty miles south of Cape Race, the ship sailed into a strong gale. With the heavy load in high seas, the ship strained and began to take on water. *Hope* listed out. The weight on deck hove the ship down on its beam ends, on its side in danger of capsizing.

At 10 a.m. the crew chopped the lashings holding the timber on deck in an attempt to set it adrift. But it didn't move, being held fast by the fore braces and ship's rigging. The bosun then took an axe to cut the fore braces. Just as he got to the lee side, the vessel settled down and with hardly a minute's warning, turned completely over.

One of the crew, Arthur Frank Jolliffee of the Isle of Wight, described what happened next: "This was 11 a.m. Monday, August 22. We all managed to get on the ship's keel, but we had only been there a few minutes when a heavy sea swept over us, carrying all into the sea. The water around the capsized *Hope* was then strewn with deals as the deck load had broken adrift when the vessel upset.

"All of us, except the mate who was never seen after he was washed off the keel, were left struggling in the water. After considerable difficulty we all managed to get on to the pieces of deals. Bosun William Rees and myself were on a piece of deal when he saw a piece of rope (the starboard fore upper brace) floating on some deals close by.

"He said, 'Now if we can get that piece of rope we can make a raft.' He succeeded in reaching it and cutting a length of rope, but it was a short piece. Rees told John Nicholas, who was floating near us on some deals, to get another piece of rope and lash the deals together."

Somehow Rees got another length of rope. All this was accomplished in high winds in choppy seas. Eight of the nine crew were adrift on the open ocean, clinging to large pieces of timber. Resourceful and determined to rescue themselves despite the terrible odds against them, they worked together to survive.

Jolliffee and Rees secured about a dozen deals and lashed them together as securely as possible under the circumstances. There was no way to maneuver the crude raft to get to the others. Jolliffee said, "We were slowly drifting away from the others who were all holding on to pieces of timber. The life-boat, which had broken adrift from the wreck, floated past us, but we were unable to reach it. We called out to able seaman Humphrey Jones to try to get it, as it was going close to him, but he could not.

"We were now on our raft of deals away from the others, but we seemed to drift back near them again. John Nicholas, having been on five deals which he had fastened together, neared us. As he did, he threw us a piece of rope which he had and we got hold of it and hauled him onto our raft. We took his deals and lashed them to ours, making in all about fourteen pieces fastened together."

Jolliffee could see only three others of his shipmates battling for life in high seas. The cabin boy, James, had disappeared. Seaman Robert Hughes was some distance off, wearing a life buoy. Jolliffee called out to him to strike out for them, as they had a raft. But he thought that Hughes couldn't hear or was too weak to make the attempt.

Cook Edwards and seaman Jones were last seen with their heads on one deal and their feet on another. Jolliffee recalled, "After awhile we lost sight of those two and only Hughes remained. He was stripped naked and struggling for his life against heavy seas. We lost sight of him when darkness came on.

"During the early part of the first evening we sighted a double topsail schooner, hove to about three miles from us. The bosun and I tried to signal to her by standing up on the raft and holding on to Nicholas, who was kneeling to keep us from falling off. A short time after, the wind chopped around and lulled. The schooner set sail and went away from us.

"The next day the wind and sea had gone down to a calm. About noon we sighted a fore and aft rigged schooner and took one of our deals and held it up for a mast. I took off my shirt and used it as a signal. We were then within a mile and a half from the schooner, but apparently they did not see us and she, too, soon disappeared."

By then the three survivors of Hope were feeling the pangs of hunger and thirst. Although they knew their relative position – off Cape Race, in shipping lanes and close to the fishing grounds of the Grand Banks – their thoughts of quick rescue were sinking fast.

On August 24 they sighted no less than three small schooners, but the raft was too far away and they sailed on. That day, Wednesday, fortunately was fine and bright, but in the evening the wind came up again. Seas again began to wash over the raft. Jolliffee remembered that Nicholas, who was thoroughly exhausted and lying down on the raft, had to be held by his mates and that "Our sufferings were then becoming terrible. Our throats were on fire and our tongues were becoming stiff. In order to alleviate our agony, I cut the straps from my sea boots into pieces and these we chewed to keep our tongues moist.

"By then we never expected to be saved and thought it was only a question of a few hours and we would follow our companions to a watery grave.

"The next morning, the 25th, three more schooners were in sight. After much exertion, we took up another long deal and rigged it up as a mast as a last effort. To our joy, our signals were seen."

It was the Lunenburg, Nova Scotia, fishing schooner Amelia C, under the command of Captain Rafuse. The survivors were weak, but the crew of the schooner got them aboard. Jolliffee said, "We had had nothing to eat or drink since Monday, August 22, at 7:30 a.m. Amelia C remained on the Banks to complete her trip." On September 16, they were landed at Halifax – three remaining from a crew of nine of the Welsh barque Hope.

# 32

## Rewarded for bravery on the high seas

*January 1893*

In January 1894, this announcement appeared in papers and in marine publications in North American shipping circles: "The Danish government awards binoculars to Captain W. Taylor of Munn & Company's brigantine *Kestrel* for rescuing two seamen in mid-Atlantic."

The rescue had actually occurred the year before. As *Kestrel* sailed in latitude 37.20 North, longitude 42.25 West on January 15, 1893, it passed the Danish brigantine *Louvisa* about one mile off. The sea was rough; the weather was typical for January, windy and cold. Captain William Taylor could see something was not right about the vessel – the way it lurched and meandered apparently out of control, the disarray of sails, the wallowing ship low in the ocean.

Taylor ordered his crew to put back and without much trouble reached the damaged brigantine. There were two seamen aboard, Hans Zaage and Hans Holte. It was they who told the woeful tale of misadventure on the Atlantic.

On the first day of January the *Louvisa* was thrown on its side, its foremast was carried away, and two men were washed from the deck, never to be seen again. There was so much water in the hold, the vessel wallowed in the troughs and crests of a wild sea. The captain, Peter Eriksen, was below and in the sudden shift of the vessel as it turned on its side, he was thrown down, dislocating his shoulder. He had to be brought up to the deck by two crewmen. He was so incapacitated, that when troubles with the ship became more serious, he was unable to endure and passed away after two days. He was buried at sea.

A short time after, another seaman died as well and to add to the trauma and hardship the cook was washed overboard. This left the two men, Zaage and Holte, to attempt to get the ship back on an even keel. This would have been an extremely difficult task had there been a full crew, but with only two weakened men, it was nigh impossible. At night they were forced to climb the rigging, lashing themselves on to avoid being washed overboard. During the day they gathered in the after part of the ship, doing what they could to work the vessel.

During their ordeal the two beleaguered seamen subsisted on very scant food, mostly a few tins of preserved meat, tinned sardines, and a little cheese. They had no bread or potatoes. The lack of water was the greatest problem. Somewhere in the ship they found a couple of bottles of wine and other spirits. This, without water or tea, actually made them feel worse instead of improving their health.

On the fifth day after the accident to *Louvisa*, they managed to catch a little rainwater. This was all they had to keep them alive until rescue came – if indeed it would come at all. One of them became weak and utterly exhausted, languishing to the point of welcoming death. The other man was not much better.

Then on January 15, a sail appeared. Zaage and Holte were too far gone even to raise proper signals of distress in the rigging. The only thing flying was a torn section of the Danish flag. Yet the discerning captain on the vessel in the distance could see something was wrong. It was fifteen days since *Louvisa* fell a victim of the sea.

Captain Taylor carried the two survivors into his home port, St. John's, Newfoundland. He later gave his report of the rescue and this was the one sent to the Danish government, informing them of the loss of *Louvisa* and that only two men of its crew had survived.

Taylor's report says: ". . . The wrecked vessel proved to be *Louvisa* of Vidi, Denmark, which sailed from Puerto Rico with a cargo of mahogany for Havre, France. A heavy sea struck the ship and laid her on her beam ends. The mate and two seamen were washed away when the foremast went overboard. . . . the captain was injured. He was pulled from the cabin and lashed to the side of the ship. . . . The cook was washed away.

"After three hours the foremast gave way to the deck and helped right the hull somewhat. The rest of the crew were compelled to take to the rigging. A colored crewman died of exposure during the night. . . . the next to go was the captain and he was committed to the deep.

"The two remaining crew managed to get into the main staysail which sheltered them as they used to wrap themselves up in it during the night. That way they got a little sleep. After two days the seas pitched down somewhat and they managed to get into the cabin and got a little food. . . . When the four bottles of liquor they found were gone, they were forced to suck moisture from the rigging and sail.

"Then when the sea became smooth, they got on top of the after cabin, cut away two planks and found a jar inside. In this they could catch a little rainwater. Everything they could get had to be taken up to the rigging and made fast.

THE LIFE-BOAT BRADFORD RESCUING THE CREW OF THE DANISH
BARQUE AURORA BOREALIS OFF RAMSGATE

A lifeboat rescues the crew of the Danish barque *Aurora Borealis* in 1867 off the southeast coast of England. In another drama on the sea, a passing ship rescued two of a crew of seven from the Danish ship *Louvisa*. (*Illustrated London News*, January 17, 1867)

". . . When rescued there were only two lanyards in the main rigging, supporting the mainmast; all the rest were chafed off. When this mainmast went overboard, the two men would have had to go with it. It was impossible to take shelter in any other part of the waterlogged vessel."

Thus was Captain William Taylor of Carbonear, Newfoundland, cited for bravery and accorded honour by the Danish government. As was the custom in those days of all-sail vessels pounding the ocean highways, the tangible reward was an item useful for sailors – binoculars. Taylor received his award in January 1894, nearly one year to the day after the rescue.

# 33

## *Mutiny of a different kind*

*July 1893*

$\mathcal{M}$utiny at sea is considered to be an open revolt against a ship's officers, culminating in the takeover of the vessel by those not in authority. The act of rebellion is either squashed by the ship's officers or the mutineers take command of the vessel, usually with fatal results to superiors.

A shipboard rebellion, or mutiny as it was termed by the St. John's *Evening Herald*, raised its ugly head on a fishing vessel in the summer of 1893. During the fishing season of the previous summer there were several complaints from fishing vessel owners of low catches, small fares, little fish in the holds when the ships returned to Gloucester and Boston. Why were catches low?

According to the captains of certain ships, their crews refused to work and did nothing but lie in their bunks. By mid-fishing season 1893, skippers and owners claimed clearly and without doubt, this refusal was a criminal action. In July, Frank Stanwood, owner of the Gloucester banker *Ellen A. Swift*, had eight of his crew arrested and charged with "the serious crime of mutiny on the high seas." *Ellen A. Swift* was under the command of Captain Solon Larkin and carried a crew of eighteen men. It had sailed for the Banks in the early spring, 1893.

When the vessel landed back home with a poor catch, tempers flared. The United States Deputy Marshall Fred D. Galloupe arrived on the deck of *Ellen A. Swift* with warrants for the arrest of eight men – Nova Scotians Albert Goodwin, Jason Blades, Stephen Larkin, David Tibbetts, Eben Larkin, Gilbert Amado, Thomas Smith who gave his address as Germany, and Thomas Hoben of Burin, Newfoundland. It is not known if the Larkins were related to the skipper.

Captain Larkin claimed his vessel was fitted out at a cost of $3,600, and bills for other sundry items and bait obtained during the trip added another $1,000. *Ellen A. Swift* returned to port on Monday after a voyage of five months with a catch of 140,000 pounds of cod, valued at $3,800; half of the value was to be divided among the crew.

Larkin claimed, "The slim amount is caused by the refusal of the crew to fish or obey the necessary orders to prepare to fish. They refused to catch bait necessary for the procuring of fish. When squid was plentiful on the Misaine Bank, only five of my crew obeyed orders to go out in the dories."

The situation was so desperate, he said, "I had go out in one of the dories in order to get three dories in operation."

While these three dories were out, the rest of the crew stood at the rails of *Ellen A. Swift*, taunting and calling derisively to the men. They shouted at the captain and asked him why he didn't take the vessel back home.

If Larkin wanted to go home, he had difficulty getting the schooner underway. The crew refused to furl the sails, weigh anchor or generally work the ship. What was happening, according to the captain, was equal to a mutiny, a downright defiance of what they were supposed to do.

But in port the accused crew would not take this "lying down," so to speak, without coming to their own defense. A spokesman stated, "The skipper acted surlily towards us all during the trip, scarcely deigning to speak or give orders. When work was to be done he rarely gave orders directly, but through one of his men.

"Our crew sailed all over the large fishing banks during the voyage and all went well during that time. The master became discouraged at the poor fare secured and lost ambition, refusing to give orders or take the necessary steps to secure a supply of bait. Here's an example.

"In the early part of August, the vessel was in Bay Bulls, Newfoundland, seeking bait. The local fishermen came on board with a supply, but as Captain Larkin was absent on shore, we did not feel authorized to buy. After the captain came aboard he was informed that bait could be obtained and was asked for authority to purchase should he be absent again.

"He replied that he had no orders to give and again left the vessel. During all this time, the bankers *Edith M. Prior, Dora A. Lawson, Mystery, Thomas F. Bayard, Samuel N. Colby* and *General Cogswell* came into port, obtained a supply of bait and departed for the Banks.

"We found our own bait on the Banks, baited our hooks and awaited the orders of Captain Larkin to get the dories out. Instead Captain Larkin sailed aimlessly about the bay for nine days. During this time the bait rotted on the hooks and had to be removed."

The last conflicting bit of evidence stated that "The captain, having made a poor voyage, endeavored to put the blame on the crew."

Six members of *Ellen A. Swift* were held as witnesses: Charles Larkin, William McCreet, Smith H. Larkin, William Kenney, Valentine Tobin and the ship's cook. One crewman to be questioned was Abijah Larkin, but he could not be found. Another young boy named Hoben was frightened by the experience. He had never been in the United States before, but was shipped in Newfoundland without signing any articles and had always obeyed orders.

The accused were to be taken to Boston, but before it came to a trial for mutiny on the high seas, an agreement was reached. The case was settled as a dispute between the captain and his crew and did not qualify as a "mutiny" as there was no takeover of the vessel. Subsequently, many of Solon Larkin's disgruntled fishermen left the *Ellen A. Swift* to go back home or to find another Gloucester banker, perhaps a more productive one.

# 34

## *An attempted rescue*

*January 1894*

Not every rescue at sea ended successfully, with a feeling of accomplishment, perhaps with awards for bravery and a well-published account of the event. There were times when the opposite happened. Not only was the attempt aborted or fruitless, but the rescue ship and its personnel ran into difficulty. This was certainly illustrated in January 1894 when the American fishing vessel *Maggie E. Wells* ran into trouble.

As so often happens in stories of the sea, an ocean storm pounded the *Maggie E. Wells*, such that the schooner became leaky and was in danger of foundering. The skipper, knowing he was in shipping lanes, ran up distress flags in hopes that some ship would come along to pluck him and the crew off his sinking vessel.

UPSETTING OF THE LIVERPOOL LIFE-BOAT ON HER WAY TO
RESCUE THE CREW OF THE LELIA

Attempting to reach the beleaguered crew of *Lelia*, the Liverpool lifeboat upset and twenty lives were lost – seven from the lifeboat and thirteen from the ship. The picture from the January 28, 1865, *Illustrated London News* shows what may have happened to the crew of the *Amsterdam* who went to rescue sailors from *Maggie E. Wells*.

At 11 a.m. on Sunday, January 11, the westbound ocean liner S.S. *Amsterdam* answered the distress call and slowly swung around toward a wallowing fishing vessel. At the time, *Maggie E. Wells* was in latitude 14.21 North, longitude 58.18 West, in moderately high seas with a strong breeze. What happened next is best described by the captain of *Amsterdam*: "We saw in the distance what appeared to be a fishing schooner, showing an American flag at half mast – a signal of distress.

"We made for the schooner and saw that the sea was washing constantly over her, and that only by hard pumping was the ship kept afloat. The crew of fourteen signaled us by gestures that the vessel was in a sinking condition, and that they were anxious to leave her, showing at the same time, by throwing overboard pieces of their boats, that they had been storm damaged.

"I called my crew on deck and told them the position in which the schooner was. Immediately the first officer and six of our crew offered themselves to man a boat and to go to their rescue.

"At about 12 noon, boat No. 4 left our steamer and everything went all right until in the vicinity of the wreck, when a sudden snow squall capsized the boat. The result was three of the crew disappeared immediately and the remaining four succeeded in taking hold of the capsized boat.

"I went at once to their assistance and succeeded in getting the capsized boat alongside, but it appeared that the remaining four men were thoroughly exhausted by the cold. They were not able to take hold of the life saving apparatus which were given them with the exception of one sailor. Seaman A. Vanderwilt, because of his extraordinary presence of mind, calm behavior and the fact that he was a good swimmer, got hold of a rope and was taken on board.

"Another crew presented themselves to man a second boat. Owning to the increasing wind and sea, I objected and concluded to wait for better weather and a calm sea. We stayed in the vicinity of the wreck until 6 o'clock when, in a heavy snow squall, we lost sight of the schooner. Although we searched two hours, we were not able to find any trace of the wreck and proceeded on to port."

S.S. *Amsterdam*, already running behind in its scheduled run to New York, had to leave the scene. Not only had the crew of the fishing vessel not been rescued, but six of seven lifeboat men had perished. Although the captain does not say, it is unlikely that even the bodies of *Amsterdam*'s deceased crew were recovered. There would be no glory or reward for the safe delivery of distressed seamen.

In the storm and heavy seas, the captain could not even positively identify the foundering schooner, saying it appeared to be *Maggie E. Wells*, and that the full name and place of registry could not be clearly read on the stern. Yet his crew, although they had just seen six shipmates perish, volunteered to try a second time to get to the sinking schooner. Added to the feelings of despondency and defeat was the thought that perhaps fourteen men had been lost on the fishing vessel.

Eventually *Maggie E. Wells'* crew was rescued by an eastbound ship and arrived in Halifax on February 1, 1894.

# 35

## We struck something, some wreck

*January 1898*

Captain James E. Dakar of the wrecked steamer *Gerona* knew his vessel was on the bottom, but he was unsure of exactly what he had struck to put it there. He and his crew left Portland, Maine, on the last day of December 1897, bound for Yarmouth, Nova Scotia.

A few hours out, Dakar saw the Yarmouth steamer *Boston*. "About 3 a.m. on January 1, just before dawn of the first day of the new year, I saw a light and judged it to be about eight miles off." That was the end of what was supposed to be a routine voyage.

The Saint John, New Brunswick, *Daily Sun* featured the loss of *Gerona*:

### WRECKED GERONA
She Went Down in Twenty-five Fathoms of Water
Capt. Dakar was in Chart Room at the Time of the Disaster

## He is of the Opinion his Vessel Struck Some Wreck, Probably the "Assaye"

The 2,035-ton Thomson liner *Gerona*, registered in Dundee, Scotland, brought cargo from the United States to Nova Scotia. On its last voyage the cargo had a value of $200,000. As he steamed northward, *Gerona*'s captain was unsure of the coastline, but knew he was close to the treacherous Blonde Rock off Seal Island in southern Nova Scotia.

The account of *Gerona*'s wreck is best told through the captain's words: "After we saw a light, we struck something. I was in the chart room at the time, and at first the only thought was we had struck an extra heavy sea. There were a couple of bumps, not very hard, and we passed.

"Then I headed south, but we found we were taking in water and on sounding found fifteen feet in her hold. Boats were ordered out. The first boat was struck by a sea and broken in two as it was being lowered, leaving the men hanging by the ropes to the davits. Then a second boat was launched with twenty men, under command of the third officer. In the resetting by the two men hanging by the davits, this boat was lifted up on a high wave and it punched a hole in the bottom of another boat.

"However, a third boat was launched, in charge of Second Officer Watson and took twenty-four men. This left fourteen men to be gotten off with only a fifteen-foot dingy to take them in. However, I managed to get them all away safely and then the boat was so overloaded that I managed to get three men transferred to the lifeboat. One boat managed to get to land on Seal Island by 10 o'clock and the other boat to the mainland at Forbes Point.

"My little boat was less fortunate. The sea was so high and the wind blowing so hard, it having freshened up considerably after we left the steamer, that after repeated attempts

Debris from an unknown wreck on Seal Island. (Photo by Captain Hubert Hall, Shipsearch Marine, Yarmouth, Nova Scotia)

to reach Seal Island we gave it up. We went to try and reach Mud Island.

"This we managed to do with great difficulty about 2 o'clock in the afternoon. I left the steamer at 4:30 a.m. and before leaving went down in the engine room and found the water up to the first platform. By this time *Gerona* was settling fast and listing considerably. I used the lead sounding line just after the wreck and found the vessel was in twenty-five fathoms of water."

By the next day, January 2, other ships went to search the area, which was determined to be off Seal Island. According to shipping authorities, *Gerona* had probably touched "The Blonde," a treacherous round rock about three miles from Seal Island. It is said to be named after the 32-gun H.M.S. *Blonde* lost on May 10, 1782, while en route to Halifax with a captured vessel in tow.

On January 1, the night of *Gerona's* stranding, the tide was full and apparently Captain Dakar backed off the rock and ran three miles to the south.

The steamer *Ulunda*, under Captain Fleming, steamed in search of *Gerona* as far south as Gull Island, where it met the liner *Halifax*. Both ships saw nothing from the wreckage of *Gerona*. Fleming steered further off the coast, keeping a lookout from the foremast all the time in clear weather. Southeast of Cape Sable Island, *Ulunda* passed a floating cask, partly submerged. It was new and apparently from *Gerona*, but no other debris could be found.

When Captain Dakar was asked to be more specific about what he hit and where, he replied: "I don't know what we struck, but I think it must have been some wreck. There has been a capsized vessel reported floating off the coast by a Gloucester fishing schooner, and the *Assaye* wreck is also off thereabouts now. The wreck of *Assaye* drifted off Blonde Rock."

*Some notable wrecks of Blonde Rock and Seal Island, southern Nova Scotia*

H.M.S. *Blonde*, England, May 10, 1782
*Assaye*, December 1897
*Gerona*, January 1, 1898
*Orinoco*, England, July 26, 1907
*Snipe*, USA, June 21, 1923
*Aberdeen*, Canada, October 13, 1923
*Josephine de Costa*, U.S.A., September 17, 1929
*Guard*, Canada, September 21, 1929
*Whiteway*, Nova Scotia, August 20, 1934
*William Macally*, 1942 (refloated)
*Fermont*, September 1992

# 36

## Panic on the liner, death on the schooner

*June 1898*

The officers on the bridge of the North German Lloyd steamer *Ems* thought they did everything right, but in the end six people died at sea. While steaming at half-speed, ten knots per hour, they blew the ship's whistle in blasts of four and six seconds at intervals of one minute. In addition, there was a lookout posted on the forecastle head and another in the crow's nest.

The *Ems* had nearly completed its westward voyage from Mediterranean ports and carried a large group of European immigrants of several nationalities to America. At 9 p.m. on June 14, 1898, it swung southward toward port and proceeded carefully while about four miles east of the Nantucket Shoals Lighthouse off Massachusetts. The weather had been very foggy for twenty-four hours, so much so the ship's officers had to navigate by dead reckoning.

Third Officer Klugkist said, "Captain Harrassowitz and I were on the bridge. At the time we heard fog signals repeated at regular intervals. The first officer took out his watch and timed the signals and they corresponded exactly to the fog signals of the Nantucket Lightship. So we naturally took it for granted they came from that lightship."

Then *Ems'* officers saw a bright light which a schooner had on the poop deck and they saw the sails about the same time. Harrassowitz realized the schooner was on the starboard tack, sailing by the wind, so he rang for full speed ahead. At the same time the helmsman threw the wheel to the starboard. Thus, thought the officers of the liner, the *Ems* would veer away from the schooner. They believed the schooner, which had all sails set, would come up before the wind and pass the *Ems* safely. It seemed to be going as fast as the liner.

"But," said officer Klugkist, "the schooner kept right on its course. There was a moment of terrible suspense and then the prow of the *Ems* crashed into the vessel amidships, running its nose right through it."

Upon impact, the mast of the schooner snapped and fell across the steamer's deck. The officers of the *Ems* kept the speed of the steamer up, keeping the two halves of the schooner clinging to the bow of the steamer. To stop the steamer would mean the severed pieces of the schooner would sink immediately.

As both ships plowed on, some of the crew on the schooner climbed the rigging which lay against the side of the larger ship and scrambled onto the deck of the *Ems*. Four reached safety this way; there were eight more yet to be accounted for. Officer Klugkist described the scene on *Ems*: "I met Fourth Officer Gartner, who had just come up from below, and both of us began throwing out life preservers. Our passengers were panic-stricken, those in steerage screaming and praying in half a dozen languages. The cabin passengers were also screaming and trying to prevent us from throwing the life preservers, saying they might need them themselves."

The schooner they struck was the *Gypsum Princess* and only four of twelve aboard were accounted for. Klugkist and another officer manned a lifeboat to look for people in the water, pulling Edward Paulsen, the schooner's helmsman, out of the water. He had been swimming in the wreckage with a broken leg. A half mile further out they found another seaman from *Gypsum Princess*, clinging to a spar and shouting for help. No other living persons could be found and *Ems* continued on its way.

*Ems* itself had received considerable damage and had two holes on the starboard side, one three feet in diameter and another, a four-sided indentation, with a crack on all four sides. Water flooded the first compartment; thus the liner's pumps had to be kept going. The captain said if *Gypsum Princess*, heavily laden with gypsum, had struck the *Ems*, instead of *Ems* striking the schooner, it would have sunk the liner.

The 664-ton *Gypsum Princess*, a tern schooner built in 1892 in Parrsboro, Nova Scotia, was owned by J.B. King and Company. Schooner and cargo were valued between $80,000 and $100,000. The schooner's second mate, Fulton Lake, said Captain David Merriam had gone down with the wreckage, but more tragic, his wife, fourteen-year-old daughter Ruth and a younger son were with him. Another older son, first mate Edgar Merriam, and the cook Sanford Murray were also presumed drowned from *Gypsum Princess*.

When the liner reached New York, Lake gave his version of the accident, but attached no blame to either his schooner or the liner *Ems*. There had been a heavy fog that had lasted for three days. At 8 p.m. on the Tuesday evening of the collision, he heard Mrs. Merriam tell her daughter it was time for bed. The little boy was already asleep in an improvised hammock in the cabin.

Lake said he was unable to get to sleep for an hour; then he heard the lookout shout, "Whistle on port bow!" This was followed by another shout, "All hands on deck! Steamer close on port bow." As Lake rushed on deck, he heard Mate Merriam repeat the warning and both saw a big steamer hurtling toward them. By this time, Captain Merriam had also come up from below and stood by helmsman Paulsen.

Captain Merriam then ran below to get his wife and two children and in the meantime the great steamer hit the schooner. But the captain reached the deck with all three loved ones. Paulsen was knocked down and had his leg broken, yet he assisted the captain in lowering the stern lifeboat. In his statement to *The New York Times* Lake said: "Then Paulsen was in the boat and Captain Merriam told his daughter Ruth to jump in. She replied, 'It's too far, Papa!' Her hesitation probably caused the loss of the family. The schooner sank then and the lifeboat was drawn down by the suction. Paulsen was tossed into the sea, but kept himself afloat despite a broken leg.

"The captain's eldest son, First Mate Edgar Merriam, was in the rigging of the main topmast. Both the mainmast and the topmast snapped off, the former falling across the steamer. Edgar was believed to have been flung into the sea.

"Lookout Bernard Hansen ran into the rigging, but lost his grip and fell into the water. He began to climb up the ropes on the side of the steamer and was finally saved. Those rescued were myself, Paulsen, Hansen, seamen William Fliz, Alfred Johansen and Churchill Parker, the donkey engine operator."

The gypsum-carrying schooner was gone. Six survived. Six perished, including Captain Merriam and his family – his wife, two sons and a daughter.

# 37

## When La Bourgoyne went down

*July 1898*

In one of the thick fogs which, in the months of June and July, hang over the Grand Banks and about Sable Island in the North Atlantic, the French liner *La Bourgoyne* collided with the sailing ship *Cromartyshire*. In less than half an hour, the cold North Atlantic waters engulfed *La Bourgoyne* and its 562 passengers and crew.

The horror of the disaster was compounded when it was learned how cruel and savage human nature becomes when life and limb are in jeopardy. The story, when it was related at the time, was horrible in the extreme. Instead of heroic conduct, the most outrageous acts of dishonour took place.

On the morning of July 4, 1898, *La Bourgoyne* crept through the fog. On board were several hundred passengers, including two hundred women of whom only one, Mrs. La Casse, survived. It was only by chance and extraordinary circumstances that she lived to tell of the disgraceful acts of certain crewmen. She also spoke of the efforts of her husband in his thoughtfulness in putting a life belt around her.

Mrs. La Casse said, "I can never forget what happened. We all scrambled on deck and a regular panic followed. The Captain and a few officers held the bridge and gave orders, but none were obeyed.

"On the port side, hanging in the davits, was a boat with forty women seated, but neither officers nor crew attempted to man the boat. The tacklings were set tight, and the women attempted to let the lines loose, but to no avail. They even tried to cut them clear by biting the ropes through, but with no result.

"Finally the vessel listed, and at such an angle that I fell over the decks and into the water. The list was so great that many others dropped into the ocean, but not being provided with life belts soon sank.

"I floated, and soon felt a strong arm draw me towards a raft. It was my husband. I had only been on the raft a few minutes when the steamer sank, and a whirlpool encircled the spot where the steamer had been floating. I watched, and a minute or so later, bodies came rushing to the surface, and with such force that they went many feet into the air. The struggle for life continued after.

"The many who had not been drawn down in the vortex attempted to reach rafts and boats, but as they did they were shot and beaten away by those who had in the meantime reached safety. In an hour all was over, and we, my husband and myself, were rescued by a small boat from the *Cromartyshire*."

Thrown into the water when the steamer listed out, Mrs. La Casse did not see what happened to the forty women seated in the lifeboat. Descriptions of ensuing scenes on deck and in that particular boat come from the narrative of a surviving male passenger: "The scenes after the collision were

On August 14, 1888, *Thingvalla* and *Geiser* collided off Sable Island, resulting in 119 deaths. In this picture from the *Illustrated London News* people are swept into the ocean from the *Geiser* as they were in the wreck of *La Bourgoyne* ten years later.

terrible to witness. Men fought for their positions in the boats like raving maniacs. Women and children were forced back and trampled on by the human beasts. On board were a lot of Italians and other foreigners who cared little for human life. Those fiends stopped at nothing. In one boat was a party of forty women, but so great was the panic that not a hand was raised to assist the launching of the boat.

"The occupants so near safety were drowned like rats when the ship, with an awful hissing sound, went down with hundreds of valuable lives. So desperate was the situation that an Italian passenger drew his knife and made a thrust at one who, like himself, was endeavoring to reach the boats. Knives were flourished and used with deadly effect.

"Women and children were driven back to an inevitable death at the point of weapons, the owners of which were experts in their use. Even the sick were not respected, and women were stabbed like so many sheep.

"The scene on the water was even worse. Many of the unfortunate women who were struggling in the water attempted to drag themselves into the boats and rafts. These were rudely pushed back to a watery grave.

"It was a time in which compassion was not to be found. Here the knives and other accursed weapons did their work."

These horrific scenes could not be seen by those on *Cromartyshire*, the other ship involved in the collision, as thick fog greatly reduced visibility. *Cromartyshire*'s crew were not witnesses, but after a few hours its lifeboats rescued the few survivors. When the men and the lone woman came on board, there were several verbal reports of the desperate knife and fist fights played out on the deck and in the waters around the sinking *La Bourgoyne*.

Five hundred and sixty-two perished in the greatest shipping disaster in the North Atlantic, only surpassed when the *Titanic* sank fourteen years later.

# 38

## "Will abandon ship" –
## The arduous leaving of Londonian

When the Johnson Line steamship *Vedamore* arrived in port, shipping authorities, owners, friends and family felt a sense of relief. It had been overdue for several days. Slated to arrive in Baltimore, Maryland, the first day or so in December 1898, Captain Bartlett finally pulled into port on December 8. The reason for the delay became clear; in addition to its own crew, *Vedamore* had aboard forty-five survivors from the steamer *Londonian*.

As far as Bartlett knew there were others still on the sinking *Londonian* and they had probably gone down with the ship. They were Captain William Lee, three of his chief officers and other seamen or cattlemen. The latter had responsibility for the live cattle being shipped on *Londonian*.

A CARGO SHIFTED – WRECK OF STEAMER HINDOO FROM NEW
YORK TO HULL AS SEEN BY RESCUE SHIP ALEXANDRIA

On this steamer, like the *Londonian*, waves break across the deck after the steamer
became leaky in heavy seas. Waves sweep everything overboard, smashing hatch
covers and damaging lifeboats. (*Illustrated London News*, March 20, 1880)

On November 15, about a week or so out of Boston, *Londonian*, a 5,000-ton ship built in 1896, ran into foul weather that quickly developed into a gale. The steamer began to take on water. A few hours later, the steering gear jammed and it became impossible to keep the ship head-on into the wind. In this vulnerable state, it broached side on to the seas and winds and soon was on its beam ends. The cargo shifted, the engine room flooded, and high waves broke over the decks. *Londonian*'s luckless crew was helpless to right the ship, and for two days it drifted about at the mercy of wind and wave.

On November 24 the crew had no choice but to jettison cargo and the 610 head of cattle were herded overboard. This had only a minimal effect on the list and the crew realized it was only a matter of time before *Londonian* went down.

In the early morning of November 25, the *Vedamore* hove in sight. It was still dark and *Londonian's* crew ran up signal fires to the top masts and fired distress rockets. As soon as *Vedamore* arrived alongside, the captain signaled his ship was standing by. Lee asked to be taken in tow, but Captain Bartlett declined to do this, as it would put both ships in jeopardy. He did agree to attempt to get a boat alongside to rescue the crew. Signals from *Londonian* read, "Will abandon ship."

Second Officer Hobbs and his brave volunteer rescue crew battled the elements for three hours, but were finally forced to return to *Vedamore*. Captain Bartlett then steamed to the windward of the doomed steamer. Bartlett tried a second method of reaching *Londonian*. His crew fired rockets with lines attached, hoping that even in the face of high winds they would reach the wreck. After several vain attempts, they abandoned these efforts. During the night the wind increased, but it was then another, the third, means of rescue was put in place. For four hours, life buoys with lines attached floated toward the *Londonian*. Finally, its crew hooked a line to which they attached a larger line. One of *Vedamore's* lifeboats was improvised as a life carrier to be hauled between the ships via a heavy rope pulley system.

The first trip was successful. Twenty-two of *Londonian's* exhausted crew were hauled up over *Vedamore's* side. As the empty boat was going back, a big sea broke over it and demolished the boat; a second wave carried away the ropes.

Bartlett and *Vedamore's* crew certainly weren't going to give up easily. Another boat under Chief Officer Doran and a set of valiant seamen went down over *Vedamore's* side, where it smashed against the hull, the crew barely escaping with their lives.

The next morning one of *Londonian's* boats was launched – this capsized and all occupants drowned. Fearing *Londonian* was about to go down at any minute, a second boat with twenty-three aboard left its side; this one reached *Vedamore* safely.

There were no lifeboats left on *Londonian* – all had been used, smashed or broken up by waves pounding the decks. The gale was constantly increasing. On the night of November 27-28, *Vedamore* cruised about in the vicinity. When daylight came, *Londonian* was nowhere to be seen. It had vanished. Captain Bartlett proceeded to Baltimore, regretting that he had not even more means and resources to pluck off the remaining seamen.

Newspapers of the day reported the loss. *The Halifax Herald* of December 9, 1898, said: "DISAPPEARED WITH TWENTY-FIVE OF CREW – Captain and Chief Officer of Londonian Supposed to Have Gone Down With Their Ship."

And the tale of hardship on the North Atlantic could only end with the question: Are the rest of the crew alive?

Meanwhile, while *Vedamore* sped to port with the survivors aboard, Captain Lee and the seven men still aboard *Londonian* were drifting helplessly with the gale. At midnight on November 28, the German steamship *Maria Rickmers* saw another flare from the distressed ship. Captain Grosch sent a boat under Mr. Lenz, the second officer, to the ship. After several hours, they had a line aboard the derelict and all those aboard were pulled to safety.

Seventeen perished, but *Vedamore* had rescued forty-five and *Maria Rickmers* had saved eight.

# 39

## Nightfall. November 8, 1900. –
## "Lash yourself to the rigging"

November 1900

The *Myra S. Weaver* left Florida on October 16, 1900, with a great cargo of lumber – 425,000 board feet, part of which was carried on deck. From the very outset of the voyage to New England, the three-masted schooner pushed through weather of the worst type. But it beat its way slowly northward until 5 p.m. Thursday, November 8, when it anchored six miles west of the Handkerchief Shoal in the Vineland Sound, off southwest Massachusetts.

*Myra S. Weaver*, a tern schooner of 498 tons, was valued at $25,000. In the fall of 1900 it was commanded by thirty-five-year-old Captain R.S. Vannaman of Philadelphia. Working the ship were Mate John Kearney of Calais, Maine; George Johnson; cook Peter Petersen; and several Scandinavian sailors:

RESCUE OF THE CREW OF THE CABER-FAIGH ON THE OWENS
SHOALS, ISLE OF WIGHT

Although this image shows the crew of the *Caber-Faigh* lashed to the rigging, it can be likened to the circumstances aboard the *Myra S. Weaver* in November 1900. (*Illustrated London News*, March 30, 1867)

Second Mate Rasmusson and Charles Magnussen of Norway, John Hejman, Finland and Axel Oggla. Also aboard the *Weaver* were two women passengers – Mary Emerson, age twenty-three, and Ella Beboe, age fifteen. Both were from Mobile, Alabama, and related to Captain Vannaman.

At nightfall November 8, it was blowing almost a hurricane. Great combers swept the deck. To ensure all made it through the night, the captain gave the order to passengers and crew alike, "Lash yourself to the rigging!"

The force of wind and wave swung the vessel back and forth on its anchor chains; finally the chains broke and *Myra S. Weaver* immediately began to drift landward. The first to pass away, from shock as much as exposure to the cold seas constantly beating over her, was Mary Emerson. Throughout the night, she grew weaker and weaker and died lashed to the rigging. Waves tore nearly all the clothing from her body.

At 3:30 a.m. November 9, the *Weaver* struck the Handkerchief Shoal and with an awful lurch, capsized and rolled over on its starboard side. The three masts went under water, carrying those still lashed to the rigging with them. Mate Kearney was plunged beneath the waves, but succeeded in holding onto exposed rigging above water. He saw five people perish – Captain Vannaman, the young girl, the cook and two seamen, Magnussen and Hejman.

Upon impact, most of the deck load of lumber broke loose. The great pieces of timber were like loose cannons, tossing and heaving in the high seas. Rather than the wood becoming lifesavers, it endangered the lives of those in the sea.

As soon as they could, Kearney and three other seamen climbed out of the maelstrom of wreckage and lumber pitching about. Kearney, after a superhuman effort, reached a position near the mizzenmast by jumping upon some of the boards from the cargo. Second Mate Rasmusson had both hands crushed between pieces of lumber, but managed somehow to hold on to debris until he reached the overturned ship.

Four survivors clung to their precarious perch until daylight. Then Captain Savage and the crew of the *City of Macon*, which passed near at daylight, saw the survivors. After two hours' hard work in small lifeboats, seamen from the *City of Macon* rescued Kearney, Rasmusson, George Johnson and Axel Oggla.

Of the eleven people aboard *Myra S. Weaver*, four survived and were brought into Boston.

# 40

## Drawing lots for death

*January 1905*

It began as a routine voyage for the thirty-four crewmen of the American steam dredge *Texas* which left Galveston, Texas, on December 12, 1904, sailing for Dantzic (Gdansk, Poland) via Southampton, England. In early January, while off the Hebrides on the northwest coast of Scotland, it ran into a severe gale that increased in force to a near hurricane, lasting for several hours.

Waves swept the decks of *Texas* and to make matters worse, the ship began to leak. For hours the crew pumped, but water steadily rose in the hold. They finally became exhausted. Captain Pinnet, a resident of Galveston, realized the waterlogged vessel would founder and ordered the crew to the boats.

They launched three – two immediately swamped in the heavy seas and the occupants probably perished within a few minutes. The third boat with thirteen survivors, one of whom was the captain, drifted for fourteen days, the last six of which they had absolutely no food or water. One man died from exposure.

The remaining twelve suffered untold agonies from exposure, the lack of food and, in moments of delirium, drank sea water. This only increased thirst and put most in mental and physical torture. According to the tale of hardship related in *The Halifax Herald* of January 17, 1905, "When they drank sea water, their bodies were covered in boils. The gale and rain continued and one of the castaways became insane. The others were hysterical and almost demented when rescued by the brigantine *Mercedes* which transferred them to steamship *Zeno*.

"Captain Pinnet said the lifeboat drifted about 500 miles from the scene of the disaster. He succeeded in restraining the men from cannibalism just before they sighted a rescue ship."

The twelve had already cast fatal lots to see who should die to sustain the others. According to the Halifax paper, "they were almost dead when rescued, but food and warmth revived them and all lived." They reached Waterford, Ireland, on January 13.

# 41

## A chronology of suffering

The *Vanname and King*, a coasting schooner which had been plying up and down the eastern American seaboard since 1866, left Charleston, South Carolina, on Tuesday, October 3, 1905. The vessel, registered in New Haven, Connecticut, carried eight crewmen under the command of Captain Maxwell. It was delivering a cargo of hard pine to New York.

By Thursday, October 5, the *Vanname and King* ran into a fall storm off the South Carolina coast. The aging workhorse wallowed about in high seas for several hours and then began to leak. Within a short time the crew started the pumps, but the engine room flooded and the pumps choked and stopped.

At 8 a.m. Friday, with its hold nearly full of water, the little *Vanname and King* listed out on its beam ends. The crew clambered up on the weather side and lashed themselves to the bulwarks. There they remained all day Friday, soaked to the skin by every sea that broke over them. They were constantly on the watch for some passing vessel.

That night the storm increased in fury and one great wave thundered aboard and broke both legs of seaman Arthur and swept seaman Grizell into the sea. Arthur's companions could do nothing to ease his sufferings, but when on Saturday the schooner turned completely over, they managed to cut his lashings and drag him onto a piece of the after house.

This became their raft, but they had no food, drinking water or shelter from the elements. It was several hours before they were all huddled together on the piece of wreckage. The bit of the exposed hull and keel of the *Vanname and King* they had just left soon drifted away. The vessel which had been their home on the sea was seen no more. That night seaman Arthur died and to relieve the overloaded raft his body was quietly and reverently dropped into the sea.

Sunday, October 8, brought a glimmer of hope when the desperate men sighted a ship in the distance. But in the gloom it passed without seeing the group of seamen huddled on their makeshift raft.

Sunday night the weather subsided and a little rain fell. Quickly and eagerly the seven men spread a small tarpaulin and the rainwater brought a little relief to the pangs of thirst. The few drops of water provided only temporary relief and Mate Chase became delirious. Soon his mind gave way entirely and he jumped into the sea.

The next victim of the terrific strain was Captain Maxwell. On Monday morning he became violently insane and followed the mate's example of self-destruction as a relief to his sufferings. The sight of two shipmates and friends involuntarily throwing themselves into the sea was too much for the ship's engineer. A few hours after the captain's death, the engineer too jumped into the sea.

Four men of *Vanname and King's* crew had now perished and the raft had been lightened considerably. The last victim was the steward or cook. He passed away on the raft late Monday night. With heavy hearts, the two remaining seamen dropped his body overboard.

Rescue came twelve hours later on Monday evening, October 9, when the lookout on the schooner *Stillman Kelley*, bound northward toward Boston, saw the little raft. The schooner soon hove alongside. The two survivors, Thomas and Warner, had to be lifted off the raft by a sling and for two days they were unable to speak or move.

The rescue took place off Cape Lookout, North Carolina, in latitude 33.10 North and longitude 76.30 West. The *Stillman Kelley* arrived in Boston on the afternoon of October 16, but the two survivors of the wreck of *Vanname and King* were too exhausted to walk or to be carried to shore right away. Each had lost thirty to forty pounds during five days of suffering and exposure.

# 42

## Small vessel, great heroism

*August 1906*

In the fall of 1906, two Gloucester, Massachusetts, fishermen were brought into St. John's, Newfoundland, by the local coastal steamer. How and why they were so far from home and their tale of hardship, endurance and heroism is a different kind of ocean saga.

The two men were Charles Malemberg and Patrick Manahan. While fishing from their dory they had lost their mother ship, the *Dora E. Lawson*, in heavy fog and were five days and nights without food and shelter. Manahan barely survived the ordeal, mainly because of the resolution and strength of his dory partner Charles Malemberg, a native of Sweden.

The banker *Dora E. Lawson*, owned in Gloucester by D.B. Smith, left that port on May 17 for a voyage to fish halibut and later sailed to the Labrador coast to complete its catch.

FISHING ON THE BANKS

In choppy seas and treacherous conditions, two fishermen haul a trawl from a dory just as Malemberg and Manahan did on that foggy August day in 1906. (*Harper's Weekly* XXXV # 1817)

It had already taken 75,000 pounds of halibut when the two men went astray in their dory. *Dora E. Lawson* was an unlucky ship in its record of dorymen fatalities. In September 1894 St. John's native John Dooley was lost and the next August twenty-one-year-old Wilson Roberts, from Antigonish, Nova Scotia, was lost from the schooner.

On August 9, 1906, the vessel was in the Strait of Belle Isle when the two men went to haul their trawls. After the fog drifted in, the men left the trawls to row back to the vessel. But it had already left to find them or the men missed their compass bearings for the schooner. Trying to find land or their ship, they rowed for the rest of the day and the following night, but couldn't even hear a foghorn from a ship nor the land. The thick fog persisted and after the second day, Manahan's strength gave out and he lay down in the bottom of the dory. After several hours he gave up hope and didn't care if he lived or died.

But Malemberg, senior to the other man, felt partly responsible for the predicament they were now in and would not let him give up. He used every ploy he knew to keep his younger companion clinging to life. The seas were heavy; occasionally high waves half-filled the dory. This added hardship gave Malemberg three difficult burdens – to bail the dory out as much as possible, to keep his friend's head and body above the water sloshing around in the dory and to steer the bow of the tiny craft into the wind.

For three more days and nights, the dory and its two weak occupants drifted over the cold seas south of Labrador. All this time they had no food and only about a gallon of water. They had consumed all their water by Monday, August 13. The day before they saw a steamer, but it was too far away to see them. The night of the 13th then was the worst – a ship had been sighted but their hopes had been dashed when it passed on and their water was all gone.

To "pile on the agony," as seamen are wont to say, that night a wind storm came on, increasing before daylight to hurricane force. By now, Malemberg too was almost exhausted. His arms were numb and nearly useless; he had no feeling in his legs. It was only by a superhuman effort that he was able to steer the dory into strong headwinds and keep reassuring his languishing comrade.

On Tuesday morning the storm subsided somewhat and a vessel came in sight. It was nearly mid-day. Somehow, an exhausted Malemberg struggled with the sail and got it aloft. It drove the craft toward the vessel. About 3 p.m. Malemberg and Manahan reached the side of a Danish barquentine – the *Vigilant*, under Captain Rasmusson, bound from Europe to the Labrador coast with a cargo of fishery salt.

Manahan was so weak he had to be hoisted aboard. The important thing was he was still alive, but barely. Rasmusson landed the men at Seal Island, Labrador, where they stayed for two weeks, recovering their strength.

In time the government coastal steamer *Virginia Lake* took them to Battle Harbour. There they connected with the S.S. *Home*, which carried them to St. John's. The American consul arranged transportation by train across Newfoundland to Port aux Basques and the Cabot Strait ferry. At Sydney, Nova Scotia, it was a simple matter to connect by train south to the United States and Gloucester.

Charles Malemberg was none the worse for his ordeal, but Manahan was a long time recovering.

# 43

## Secret of the sea solved after seven years

*September 1910*

When the German steamship *Pallanza* rammed a whale in the mid North Atlantic, it helped solve a seven-year mystery. In early September 1910, Captain Fendt docked the *Pallanza* in Philadelphia, having completed a voyage from Hamburg, Germany.

According to the captain's report, it wasn't a routine voyage. Somewhere in mid-ocean, his ship struck a large whale and had nearly cut the mammal in two pieces. It was a large whale and only died after a long, hard struggle. The carcass remained fixed on the bow of the steamer, slowing the forward progress of *Pallanza*. Captain Fendt stopped his vessel and lowered nine members of the crew down to chop away the whale impaled on the bow. One of the sailors found a harpoon lodged in the great mammal.

Tales of mariners relate how the great mammals often turned on the long boats and the larger whaling ships. (*Royal Readers* No. 3, 1892)

Fendt examined the harpoon and found on the end an iron band stamped "J.T.D. 1902." The captain, who kept a close and fairly accurate record of North Atlantic ships and wrecks, concluded that the whale may have been responsible for the loss of the whaler *James T. Duncan*.

The *Duncan*, termed a little whaler and carrying a crew of seven, sailed from Halifax, Nova Scotia, in the spring of 1903 and had never returned to port. Captain Fendt said, "I think it perfectly safe to say that the *Duncan* drove this weapon into the whale and in the struggle which followed was sunk by a blow from the infuriated monster."

# 44

## No help from the sea

There is a universal law, albeit an unwritten code of the sea, which says that if a ship needs help you give it. Sailors and fishermen, realizing all too well the demands and claims of the relentless ocean, believe a rescue favour will someday be returned.

There are hundreds, perhaps thousands, of rescue stories told by distressed sailors of ships that have sped to immediately render all aid possible to a sinking vessel. Rarer are the tales where the reverse happened – a passing ship draws near, sees and hears the distress and chooses to leave the scene. No aid. No rescue. Not even acknowledgment of the situation.

That was the case on October 13, 1910. It was a tale told by Captain George L. Holden when he arrived in Boston. His schooner, the three-masted *Florence Leland*, sailed for Philadelphia from Ingramport, Nova Scotia, in early October. It carried a full load of two million laths, boards and strapping, which virtually made the craft unsinkable. *Florence Leland* was a mass of wood and unlikely to run into difficulty on a relatively short run – but it did. A hurricane saw to that.

Captain Holden had four crewmen. Mate Bartlett Robbins was from Rockland, Maine; cook Charles Vincent came from Boston. Seaman Myron Dow hailed from the same place as the captain, Deer Isle, Maine. Seaman Richard Grass was probably related to the managing owner of the schooner, A.O. Grass of Deer Isle. Grass had his cargo insured, but carried no insurance on the vessel itself, valued at $9,000.

On October 8, only a few days out of port, Captain Holden and his crew sailed into a fall hurricane. By the next day winds had carried away the foremast and opened seams in the hull. In short order *Florence Leland* took on water faster than it could be pumped out and the schooner became waterlogged.

Four days later water and food, meant to last a week or so, ran out. The *Leland* had settled so deep that its cabin was filled with water. Even if there had been food, there was no way to get below to reach it nor was there any way to make a fire in the cabin stove. With the vessel so deep in the water, every wave washed over the deck, forcing the crew to lash themselves to the bulwarks or rigging. But the crew knew they were in shipping lanes and could signal "distress" to a passing ship should one appear. Although there was no danger of the schooner sinking quickly, Holden decided to abandon *Florence Leland*. There was no way he could get it to port.

In the night of October 13 they hoisted a burning tar barrel into the rigging and the glare attracted a vessel – rescue was at hand!

A great steamer, possibly a passenger liner, came down closer and circled the wallowing schooner. Captain Holden called out that he wished to abandon ship. There seemed to be no response from the steamer's bridge. Holden became more specific in his pleas: "This ship is waterlogged and we cannot get to port. We wish to be taken off." The liner stood off, about two to three hundred yards away. There was no movement toward rescue and in a few minutes the potential rescue vessel rang Full Speed Ahead, moved forward, and soon disappeared into the night.

While it was near, Holden and his crew could see passengers along the rails. Indeed much to their chagrin, the passengers, as the ship slowly moved away, stood on the rail, waved their hands and shouted, "Good-bye!" From the direction in which the ship was headed, Holden thought it was bound for the Azores.

Holden and his crew could not see the name well in the dark, but thought the first letter of the liner's name was a "V" and the last letter, "O." The words showing the ship's place of registry below the name seemed to be Italian.

The strange behaviour of the liner was the exception rather than the rule, for the very next vessel that came within range acted more humanely. Three days later – October 16, 1910 – the liner *Cedric* rescued the five desperate mariners. They were taken to Liverpool where the American consul at that port arranged transportation back to the United States.

With the exception of Captain Holden, who remained in Boston to report to the vessel's agents, most of the crew sailed to Bangor, Maine, on the steamer *Camden*. *The Boston Herald* reported the strange incident with its banner: "LEFT FIVE ON A SINKING SHIP Ignored Pleas of Men Lashed on Waterlogged Schooner to Rescue Them."

# 45

## Eleven great ships to the rescue

October 1913

There are tales of the sea that have no parallel in marine records. The burning of the *Volturno* in mid-Atlantic was a spectacular scene of marine drama.

In 1913 wireless telecommunications was playing a leading role in the dramas and tragedies of the ocean. In the spectacle of the fire aboard *Volturno*, radio called ships to the aid of a stricken liner. What appeared at her side was a fleet of some of the ablest and largest steamers and they stayed in the area for twenty-four hours, yet they were nearly helpless to assist the burning vessel or to rescue the imperilled passengers and crew.

The steamship *Volturno*, an iron cargo/passenger boat of 3,581 tons and 375 feet in length, had been built in 1906 by Fairfield Shipbuilding & Engineering Company in Glasgow, Scotland. It was administrated by the Canadian Northern Steamship Company, a firm dealing with transport of immigrants between Rotterdam and the United States.

On October 9, 1913, the call for help brought eleven ships to the side of *Volturno*, afire in the North Atlantic, about six hundred miles east of the position where R.M.S. *Titanic* went down. In the fall of 1913, the sinking of the *Titanic* was still a recent news story, having occurred eighteen months before. Headlines shouted around the world of the tragedy that befell the grandest, the most elaborate ship of them all – supposedly unsinkable. No doubt the rescue, or lack of rescue, of *Titanic's* passengers and crew was fresh on the minds of commanders and seamen alike as they raced to the aid of a fellow steamer.

But unlike *Titanic*, *Volturno* didn't strike an iceberg; fire killed 136 of its 654 occupants. As well, *Volturno* was not a highly publicized "unsinkable" vessel transporting glamorous passengers on its maiden voyage. It was simply an average-sized ocean liner making one of many trips across the Atlantic between Europe and North America. The passengers of the *Volturno* were neither wealthy industrialists nor well-known socialites. They were poor immigrants from Eastern Europe and Russia coming to America for a better life.

*Volturno*, commanded by Captain Inch, sailed from Rotterdam on October 2 for Halifax and New York. One week later, early in the morning someone discovered a blaze in the forward hold. A passenger who first saw the smoke says he thinks the fire might have been caused by a cigarette dropping through a hole in the steerage floor and upon the immigrants' luggage stored beneath.

When the ship's offi-
cers sought to check the fire,
flames were leaping forty
feet above the deck. Unfortu-
nately, there was much flam-
mable material in the cargo,
which included large quantities of oil, rags, burlap and
chemicals. Six lifeboats were
launched into a sea lashed by
a violent storm. Four of the
boats were smashed against
the ship's side, and those
who were aboard them per-
ished. Two boats got away,
but were never found.

| *Ships which helped rescue Volturno's crew and passengers* | |
| --- | --- |
| Carmania I rescued | 11 |
| Grosser Kurfürst | 105 |
| Czar | 102 |
| Kroonland | 90 |
| Devonian | 59 |
| Seydlitz | 46 |
| La Tourraine | 42 |
| Minneapolis | 30 |
| Narrangansett | 29 |
| Rappahannock | 19 |
| Asian stood by | |

Eleven ships responded to a call for help. The majority
of them were on their way to or from Europe and, putting on
full steam, they sped toward the burning vessel. The first to
arrive was *Carmania I*, as it was only seventy-eight miles away.

Within a day other great ships were near *Volturno*. But
the sea was so rough that for many hours their efforts to
do something, to rescue, to render help, were in vain. Captains sent out boats at great risk, but in the raging seas and
high winds, they were forced to return without reaching the
burning ship. Through the night a searchlight played upon
*Volturno*. Captains, seamen and passengers on the would-be
rescue ships could see panic-stricken passengers assembled
near the stern.

In the morning the sea was calmer. The gale had gone
down and the waves had been calmed somewhat by oil dis-
charged from a tanker ship hovering nearby. By then rescue
boats were able to reach the terrified passengers and crew,
who were distributed throughout several rescue ships, accord-

ing to which lifeboats reached *Volturna*. *Carmania* rescued eleven people, yet *Grosser Kurfürst* lifeboats took off 105.

Many survivors landed in New York where the leading papers of the day published their tales of suffering and danger. It was said that "never had a scene so appalling in mid-ocean been witnessed by so many spectators," for the ships that came to save lives surrounded the burning *Volturno* and stood by sixteen hours without actually plucking anyone off.

Captain Causain of *La Tourraine* sent his observations to the French Trans Atlantic Company. He said when his ship arrived in the vicinity of *Volturno*, "The forward part of the *Volturno* looked to me like an incandescent brazier. As the sea was beginning to moderate I thought of putting out boats, but the opinion of all my officers was against the lowering of lifeboats. I sent out a whaleboat, however. By this time the *Volturno* had her stern in the air, while forward and amidships it was nothing but a great torch."

Another report came from *La Tourraine*'s First Lieutenant Izenic: "It was half past eight on Thursday morning when we received the first wireless message that the *Volturno* was burning. At that time we were two hundred miles away. We reached the *Volturno* at 9 o'çlock in the evening and found ten other steamers already on the scene.

"Heavy smoke was streaming away from the forward hatches of the *Volturno*, whose passengers had assembled in the after part of the ship. The women and children had been placed farthest from the fire, while the men formed a line nearest to the point of danger.

"Everything on board the *Volturno* appeared quiet and under organized control. I could observe the crew working steadily with the hose, pouring water into the hatches from which red-tinged smoke was issuing. It was obvious from our bridge that the efforts of the crew of the *Volturno* to extinguish the fire were futile, as the flames rapidly gained strength.

"Twenty men among our passengers, who were yachts-men or otherwise familiar with the sea, volunteered to help man the lifeboats, but their services were not needed."

Lieutenant Izenic reported that upon his ship's arrival at the side of the *Volturno*, the vessel presented a frightful spectacle, blazing, plunging and rolling in the seas. Crew and passengers had been driven by the flames and smoke to the rear of the vessel, where they uttered incessantly cries of terror.

*La Tourraine's* whaleboat stood off, its crew calling to the passengers to jump into the sea, when they would be taken on board. None, however, would jump until a gigan-tic wave threw the whaleboat against the *Volturno's* side. Instantly a number jumped or slid down the ropes into the boat. Two who had jumped for the boat disappeared under the side of the *Volturno* as she rolled. One man landed on a sailor in the whaleboat and injured him.

There are conflicting reports about the behaviour of the crew and the condition of the lifesaving equipment aboard the steamer. Like the *Titanic* there weren't enough lifeboats to accommodate everyone aboard *Volturno*. Captain Inch, whose conduct was later deemed "heroic," said the crew's conduct in very trying circumstances was above reproach. There was no panic.

On the other hand, surviving passengers contended that the crew attempted to monopolize the boats and that the captain forced them back with a pistol. One of the stewards on the steamer reported the fire hose was rotten and that the boats were so leaky they filled with water when launched.

Among those who perished were several who leaped overboard, preferring death by drowning to death by fire. A young couple from France, recently married, committed suicide in this way, clasped in each other's arms.

In the early days of wireless communications, the rescue of eighty percent of the passengers of the *Volturno* was an impressive demonstration of the value of new technology. The spectacle of several great steamers rushing to the rescue of an endangered comrade is as inspiring as it is thrilling.

# 46

## Salvagers at the City of Sydney

*March 1914*

In the history of marine shipping in the North Atlantic, there were more than forty vessels named "City of . . . " Many were owned initially by the Inman Line, which was formed in 1850 by three partners, one of whom was William Inman. The shipping line catered to the immigrant trade. After several name changes and financial intricacies, the company went into voluntary liquidation in October 1886 and its remaining assets were purchased by other businesses.

The annals of North Atlantic travel are fraught with episodes of disaster, suffering and death, and the Inman fleet was likewise marked with catastrophe. Two of the most unfathomable mysteries involved Inman ships which simply disappeared, leaving not a trace behind to indicate the cause of their loss.

THE CITY OF LIMMERICK STEAM-SHIP, FOR TRAFFIC BETWEEN
LONDON AND BRAZIL

The 1,339-ton Royal Mail Steamship *City of Limmerick* on its first voyage in September 1867. In 1881, with forty-three persons on board, it disappeared completely. (*Illustrated London News*, November 23, 1867)

The *City of Glasgow* was the first Inman vessel and it traded between Glasgow and New York. A beautiful Clyde-built craft of 1,600 tons, the ship was thought to be able to withstand even the worst furies of the Atlantic Ocean. In addition to its engines, *City of Glasgow* could carry an enormous amount of canvas. The crew numbered seventy and there was accommodation for more than five hundred passengers.

It left port in early March 1854 with 480 people and was never heard of again. For mere numbers of lives lost, the *City of Glasgow* holds the Atlantic record among steamers which have simply disappeared, although collision with other ships, icebergs and rocks have caused greater loss of life.

"Magnificent" was a word commonly used to describe Inman's *City of Boston*, a well-built ship and the top of its class. In early January 1870, with every prospect of a speedy and safe voyage, it left port and plunged to the bottom somewhere in the North Atlantic, resulting in the death of 177 passengers and crew. No one ever learned why or exactly where it happened.

Several "City of" ships were wrecked on the shores of North America. *City of Philadelphia* never made it past its maiden voyage – lost on the rocks near Cape Race, Newfoundland. Cape Sable, Nova Scotia, claimed *City of Washington* for its own in 1873. For loss of life on or near North American shores, the wreck of *City of Monticello* was significant; thirty-nine people from Nova Scotia and New Brunswick perished off Yarmouth, Nova Scotia.

On March 17, 1914, the *City of Sydney* stranded on Shag Rock near the dreaded Sambro Ledges in the approaches to Halifax

## "City of" ships meet disaster

*City of Pittsburgh*, burnt out at Valparaiso, Chile, 1852, no loss of life

*City of Glasgow*, vanished in 1854 bound for Philadelphia from Liverpool, England, with 450 aboard

*City of Philadelphia*, wrecked near Cape Race, Newfoundland, on maiden voyage in 1854, no loss of life

*City of New York* (first of name) in 1864 wrecked near Queenstown, no loss of life

*City of Boston*, went missing at sea in 1870 with a loss of 177 lives

*City of Brussels*, in 1883 collision in Mersey River, loss of ten lives

*City of Montreal*, burned at sea in 1887, no loss of life

*City of Chicago*, wrecked off Ireland in 1892, no loss of life.

*City of Monticello*, wrecked in 1900 near Yarmouth, Nova Scotia, thirty-nine perished

*City of Sydney*, wrecked at Halifax in 1914, two Nova Scotia men drowned while salvaging it.

*City of New York* (third of name), wrecked near Yarmouth, Nova Scotia, 1952, no loss of life harbour. The steamer, chartered to the Red Cross Line, was bound from New York to Halifax and was slated to steam to St. John's, Newfoundland. When the action around the wreck was over, the local papers called it "as stirring a drama that has been staged on these coasts in recent years."

There was no danger to the passengers and crew of the *City of Sydney* and all had been taken off without mishap. By the next day a half dozen salvaging tugs and small steamers were trying to reach the 1,653-ton vessel. Frustrating them were the high seas and breakers, but more annoying were the scores of local lifeboats and fishermen's dories, each getting freight and salvage materials despite very risky conditions.

Time and time again the ropes broke as the dories took cargo from the forward part of the wreck and the little vessels were carried near the rocks. Some salvage craft had given up the quest in view of a southeasterly gale that was coming on; the remaining few made every effort to get what they could from the wreck before the storm broke in earnest.

About 5 o'clock in the evening tragedy struck. All told, the drama lasted twenty minutes, but in the end two lives were lost and three others came close to perishing. The entire scene was played out before the eyes of those on the steamers lying close to the wreck. The larger salvage tugs were unable to maneuver closer to the wreck site.

Captain Dan Burns, a mariner well-known along the Halifax waterfront, and Robert Snow, a seaman on the steamer *Dufferin*, were getting cargo from *City of Sydney*'s number two hatch when a wave broke, upsetting their dory. They clung to the side, but each wave brought them nearer to death on the churning waters and crags of Shag Rock.

William Snow, a cousin of Robert, was nearby in a dory alone and edged close enough that both men climbed aboard. The next wave, a high cross swell, upset the dory and all three were thrown into the water. Burns and Robert Snow were entangled in some way under the boat, but William, who had climbed onto the bottom of the dory, managed to free his cousin. Captain Burns, trying to cling to the boat, was well-nigh exhausted.

All around were other potential rescuers, lining the sides of steamers or standing on the deck of the wreck. No one could get a small boat out into the boiling seas. Dozens of men could see the drowning three, and although they shouted encouragement could do nothing.

The first move came from the Diamond liner *Cabot*, about a quarter-mile away. One of this ship's lifeboats was lying alongside laden with salvage and on deck the whole crew watched the drama. *Cabot*'s Chief Officer Mooney shouted that he couldn't bear to stand by and see those men drown. "Who'll come with me?" he asked and he jumped into the boat. Engineer Freeman, Second Engineer Bonner and a seaman followed and the lifeboat, soon cleared of its cargo, headed slowly toward the capsized dory tossing in the surf.

Meanwhile, Captain William Murdock of the steamer *Dufferin* was standing on the deck of *City of Sydney*, perhaps surveying the wreck and the salvage of its goods. He enlisted the aid of Herbert Evans, a Newfoundland seaman and a deckhand on the tug *Cabot*, and both jumped into the nearest small craft. Murdock backed the boat down to the overturned dory. Evans stood in the stern.

Others on the *City of Sydney* shouted encouragement to the drowning seamen or the would-be rescuers. A few salvagers, more experienced or practical than the rest, smashed in the heads of oil casks and poured the contents overboard. This had some effect on smoothing the breaking whitecaps, but Murdock and Evans still had a battle to save their own lives and that of three others.

When they reached the overturned boat, Herbert Evans hauled William Snow on board. Robert Snow, exhausted by his long immersion in cold water, had sunk, but Burns was clinging to the bow. Evans grabbed his collar and started to

VESSELS ASHORE IN BATTEN BAY, PLYMOUTH SOUND, DURING
THE LATE GALE

The *Illustrated London News*, November 13, 1880, reported that several vessels went ashore in Batten Bay, England, during a gale. Like the predicament at the *City of Sydney* wreck site, small vessles stood off and salvagers waited to do their work.

lift the longshoreman in when a sea forced the dories apart. Burns was wrenched from the young Newfoundlander's grasp and sank for the last time.

Both dories were within a few feet of the rocks. Seizing a pair of oars, Evans added his efforts to the fight for safety. Twice the craft almost submerged in great seas, and each time the anxious watchers saw the dory turn almost on end.

By this time the *Cabot* lifeboat was on the scene and came to the aid of Murdock and Evans. When survivor William Snow and his two rescuers finally climbed aboard *Dufferin*, it headed into Halifax to get the exhausted men to hospital.

Captain Burns, a man of about forty-five with a family, resided in Black Court off Lockman Street, Halifax. William and Robert Snow, the latter married with a family, both resided in Ecum Secum, a village north of Halifax. Sadly, a brother of Captain Burns was cook on the *Dufferin* and was standing at the rails of the wrecked *City of Sydney*. He saw the whole tragedy unfold before his eyes.

In a newspaper report of the tragedy, Captain Murdock said he and Evans got a dory and took one man off. Others who witnessed Murdock's gallant effort were loud in his praise, including Captain Harrison, the marine superintendent of the Furness Withy Company. Harrison stated the feat was the bravest thing he had ever seen and steps should be taken to recommend Murdock, Evans and William Snow for the Carnegie Lifesaving Medal.

# 47

## *Hurry up! We are on fire!*

The first indication of trouble at sea came in the evening of May 3, 1914, through the wireless signals received by Marconi operators in the eastern United States, in Canada and at Cape Race, Newfoundland. The station on Sable Island was the closest to the reported position and the operator relayed the message to mainland Nova Scotia. Later in the evening, there was a flurry of messages, giving scant details of a ship on fire in the Atlantic. The last, "Hurry up we are on fire," came from the stricken ship itself.

But about the same time, ships on the Atlantic had discovered a steamer on fire from stem to stern and with no sign of life on board. The steamer *Seydlitz*, from Bremen to New York, was steaming along about three hundred miles south of Cape Race, saw the smoke and ventured near. *Seydlitz* stopped at latitude 41.27 North, longitude 51.07 West.

When the steamer approached close enough, it learned the stricken vessel was the *Columbian*. It was the second time in less than a year *Seydlitz* had come to the aid of a burning ship. It had also responded to the distress calls of *Volturno* in October 1913.

*Seydlitz* immediately called by wireless for assistance and response came from *Franconia*, fifty miles eastward and bound for Boston, and *Olympic*, two hundred miles to the west. Later in the evening of May 5, a second message confirmed the identity of the burning ship: "Thirteen survivors of the British steamer *Columbian*, which caught fire on Sunday night, were picked up today by the Cunard liner *Franconia*, bound from Liverpool for Boston."

By the next day, reports stated the steamer *Manhattan* had found a second lifeboat carrying Captain McDonald and thirteen members of *Columbian's* crew. Two lifeboats out of three had been found. *Manhattan*, *Franconia*, *Seydlitz* and other steamers in the general vicinity continued the search for the third. Aboard were *Columbian's* first and second officers and thirteen seamen.

Bound from Antwerp to New York, *Columbian* caught fire on Sunday, May 3. Flames spread quickly and were followed by explosions. In the haste to abandon the steamer, the forty-two officers and crew had no time to provision the three lifeboats properly. Ill-prepared and with some men scantily clad, they faced a battle with the sea in open boats.

The first survivors, suffering from exposure, were picked up by *Franconia* thirty-six hours after *Columbian* was abandoned; the second lifeboat with Captain McDonald and his group was adrift more than fifty hours before the *Manhattan* found them. That left one more boat, containing fifteen men, unaccounted for. A dozen ocean liners searched for five days within a wide radius of the position where *Columbian* burst into flames.

Hope of finding the third boat dwindled, especially in light of the series of ocean storms that swept the North Atlantic. To seafaring men it seemed impossible that a small boat could pass through the storms. For the large liners, schedules had to be kept; the search wound down and they continued their journey to North Atlantic ports.

But the old adage "There is hope from the ocean, but none from the grave" proved itself. Death on land and burial in the earth has finality, but on the ocean there is some hope a crew may have survived or may have been picked up by a passing ship. On May 16, the United States revenue cutter *Seneca* found the last lifeboat. It had been adrift for thirteen days.

There were four men – the first officer and three sailors – alive and they told a tale of suffering where bodies had gone past the limit of human endurance. Eleven had succumbed to injuries and privations, and their bodies had been put overboard in order to lighten the craft.

The survivors lived on only a few biscuits and a cask of water which had long since been exhausted. At first the boat was right in the path of transatlantic traffic. They had seen three steamers in the first two days adrift. Expecting, then, to be picked up at any hour, they were not as careful with their meagre supplies as might be expected.

The water and biscuits lasted the first week; then death set in. As one after another of the castaways died, Chief Officer Teire had the corpses put over the side. By the seventh or eighth day, they searched for biscuit crumbs that had fallen in the bottom of the boat. On this, and shoe leather which provided some moisture when chewed, the men managed to survive. Finally the few survivors abandoned all expectations that their boat would be found and prepared themselves to die.

Accounts of ships or crews found after being missing for many days on the ocean were carried by newspapers of the day. The *Fishermen's Advocate* of December 4, 1915, says "There Is Hope From The Ocean." One crewman of the schooner *Madonna* spent three days clinging to a rock before he was discovered.

The boat, drifting about 120 miles to the north of where *Columbian* was abandoned, went farther and farther out of the track of ocean liners and into an area occasionally frequented by fishing schooners. Merchant ships and trading schooners avoid the immediate vicinity of Sable Island in winter and spring and, apart from ice patrol ships going to and from Halifax, no craft would be in that area.

But at that time and place, the *Seneca* was on ice patrol. As the lookout scanned the horizon for bergs, he sighted a small boat through his binoculars, although no sign of life could be seen. *Seneca* put on all speed and ran down near the lifeboat, only to discover four bodies, seemingly lifeless, lying on the bottom of the boat. The emaciated and haggard four were gently lifted to the deck of the cutter and crewmen forced warm brandy between parched lips.

All needed hospital care as soon as possible and *Seneca* rushed to Halifax, the nearest port. By May 12 the survivors were recovering in the Victoria General Hospital and progress reports said they were "doing well, cheerful" and could see visitors for short periods.

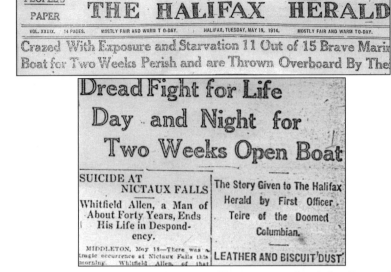

After fourteen days adrift four of *Columbian*'s fifteen men were found alive. The good news of safe deliverance was overshadowed ten days later by an even greater ocean horror – the loss of the *Empress of Ireland* and 1,100 lives on the St. Lawrence River. (*The Halifax Herald* May 19, 1914)

Although the survivors were too weak to tell the complete story, they were able to report that when *Columbian* caught fire and exploded, some of the fifteen men were badly burned from the fire. These men died in the lifeboat within a few days. Some who had tumbled from their bunks at the first explosion rushed on deck half-clothed. They succumbed to the cold quickly. Others, weakened by starvation, thirst and exposure, gradually sank into a death-like lethargy.

Somehow the survivors managed to keep the boat head-on to the seas when the weather became rough, but eventually exhaustion weakened them and they made no effort to guide the lifeboat. Day by day the number dwindled until four sank to the bottom of the boat to await the end.

# 48

## Only a day's steam from port

May 1914

 $\mathcal{M}$uch has been written of the sinking of Empress of Ireland on May 29, 1914. Pages of investigative reports, many articles and several books describe how the 8,070-ton passenger liner collided with the Storstad near Father Point in the St. Lawrence River. Eleven hundred lives were lost. Not so well-known is a shipwreck which claimed the lives of everyone aboard the Halifax Lightship 19 on Liscomb Shoals off Nova Scotia six days before the Empress of Ireland disaster. Halifax Lightship 19 received far less ink and public scrutiny.

No doubt the fishermen of Liscomb, Nova Scotia, safe in their warm homes, bemoaned the hard luck of that day in not being able to get to their lobster traps. Dense fog and heavy south winds often visit Liscomb Island and the nearby ledges. The fishermen had no idea of a terrible battle with

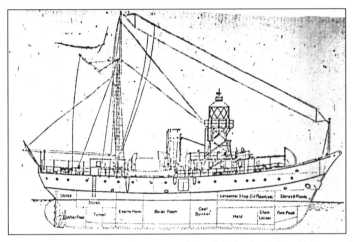

A sketch of *Halifax Lightship 19* – the revolving light is situated amidships on the little steamer.

the sea happening right on the fishing grounds in the early morning hours of May 23.

*Halifax Lightship 19*, a little steamer, was newly built in Scotland especially for Halifax harbour and had nearly completed its journey to Halifax when it struck Liscomb Ledges during a storm. The lightship, to be permanently stationed off Sambro, was the best equipped craft of its kind in the world.

Nothing was known of the wreck until Saturday morning, about 9:15, when the steamer *Dufferin*, commanded by Captain William Murdock (the same man who had figured prominently in a sea rescue on the *City of Sydney*), slowly groped along in thick fog, trying to get into Liscomb harbour. The lookout called that the vessel was moving through debris that seemed to be wreckage from a vessel. Then among pieces of timber and sections of a ship were lifeless bodies, three of which were recovered by Captain Murdock and *Dufferin's* crew.

Headlines report all sixteen lives lost on *Halifax Lightship 19.*

By this time the fishermen were out in their boats and recovered four more bodies. The government steamer *Stanley* searched the area in the evening and discovered that the wreckage belonged to the *Halifax Lightship 19.* A large section of the vessel was on its side near Crook's Ledge at the eastern end of Liscomb Island. Captain Blois of the *Stanley* and other shipping authorities figured there were six to eight bodies still unaccounted for.

Two days later the report from the search vessel concluded: "The vessel itself is beyond recovery. *Halifax Lightship* had turned completely over, smashing everything to splinters, leaving the decks literally bare of all rigging, smoke stack, davits and deck houses. The ship had struck on its starboard side and keeled over. Two other bodies were found on the island. Bruising indicated death had come to most from being dashed against the rocks rather than drowning. The lightship is as light as an egg shell, said Captain Blois, and would soon be pounded to pieces on the reef."

Later, two smashed lifeboats were found and boats coming into Liscomb reported the shore strewn with wreckage. Marine department officials at Halifax said *Lightship 19* was due into Halifax on May 23 from Glasgow, Scotland. It had sailed safely for most of the journey, but was wrecked south of its intended destination and just a few hours from Halifax.

How Captain MacBeath and the lightship came to the area off Liscomb, situated about one hundred miles south of Halifax, would never be known. It could only be speculated that the captain was looking to get in out of the heavy weather or the vessel may have been short of coal.

# 49

## Misled zeppelin meets the S.S. Franz Fischer

*February 1916*

There were many strange stories of the sea that drifted back to the North American coast during the Great War at sea. Generally, they were tales of wooden vessels and iron steamers intercepted and sunk by enemy warships or U-boats. Many stories were the accounts of lives saved or lost while running a deadly ocean gamut between storms and bombs.

But one World War I sea story centred on merchant mariners (those who served on merchant ships carrying supplies to England or Europe) aboard the collier S.S. *Franz Fischer*. While delivering coal, it was bombed in the mouth of the Thames River in England, becoming the only ship to have the misfortune to be sunk by an enemy dirigible or air balloon. Dirigibles were often called zeppelins, after the German inventor Ferdinand Von Zeppelin, and were similar to the infamous *Hindenburg* passenger airship, which crashed and burned in New Jersey in 1937, taking thirty-six lives.

During the Great War they had a more sinister use. In February 1915, the enemy deployed zeppelins to drop bombs on English cities. By April the use of airships for aerial reconnaissance by the Germans increased. They were only stopped with the introduction of airplanes, which shot them down, and when ground-to-air defense improved.

In February 1916, several enemy airships were slated to bomb Liverpool when a windstorm blew them off course and over the west coast of England. As ill-luck would have it, one zeppelin drifted near the 224-foot-long S.S. *Franz Fischer*, a captured enemy vessel employed out of England as a coasting collier. While *Franz Fischer* was anchored in the Thames estuary, the enemy sighted the lone ship and dropped a bomb on the collier. It sank in less than a minute. Of the eighteen crew, there were only three survivors: Chief Engineer Birch, cook Taylor and Charles Hillier of Newfoundland.

From his hospital bed Hillier related his story of the tragedy: "We heard a noise overhead and presently a zeppelin dropped a bomb which fell near the engine room. The vessel remained afloat only a short while."

Hillier said there was no time to do anything, put on a life jacket, launch a lifeboat. Many of the crew went under with the ship. "I survived," he said, because "when I came up to the surface I caught hold of a life belt. After swimming for sometime, I came across the chief engineer and Taylor who had managed to get hold of a life belt. By this we were able to keep afloat for an hour.

"It was pitiful to hear the cries of other men who had come to the surface after the vessel disappeared. But soon their cries ceased and we concluded all had perished. Meanwhile we continued shouting for help. When we were almost exhausted a steamer heard us, lowered a boat and picked us

## LONDON, February 3.—The Central News states that a collier has been sunk by a Zeppelin, thirteen men being drowned.

### Huns Admit Failure of Turkish Campaign in Caucasus

LONDON, February 3.—German sources admit the failure of the Turkish campaign in the Caucasus, says a Central News despatch from Amsterdam.

There has been heavy fighting ten miles south of Erzerum, where the Turks sent reinforcements from Trebizond, according to the despatch. The Turks are declared to have fought stubbornly, but were compelled to retreat.

Eighty wounded Turkish officers and five thousand wounded men have arrived at Trebizond, the message adds.

### Only Three Saved When British Steamer Was Sunk

LONDON, February 3.—The British steamer Franz Fischer, of London, has been sunk. Of her crew only three men were saved. Chief Engineer Birch, Steward Taylor, and Seaman Hillier.

### Charles Hillier, Newfoundland, a Survivor Tells of Zeppelin Sinking the Franz Fischer

LONDON, February 3.— The col- appearance of the vessel, but soon her Franz Fischer, which left Hart- their cries ceased and we concluded last Monday afternoon, was sunk all were drowned. Meanwhile we

News of the day out of Britain says, "Only three survivors when a steamer was sunk by an airship."

up. Subsequently, we were transferred to a mine sweeper which landed us."

When he was asked how a zeppelin flying from Germany managed to locate his vessel in the dark, Hillier said *Franz Fischer* was riding at anchor and her anchor lights must have been seen by the zeppelin's crew. Since the collier was stationary, it was easy to drop a bomb on it. According to news reports of the day: "*L-19* was one of nine zeppelins despatched just before noon on February 1, 1916, from Germany to bomb Liverpool. Captain Loewe and his fifteen men aboard *L-19* were charged with delivering five thousand pounds of bombs on Liverpool.

"The nine raiders lost sight of each other as darkness fell and seemed unaware that a strong southerly wind was pushing them far from Liverpool. *L-19* finally crossed the English coast near Norfolk at 7:20 p.m. Captain Loewe was heard by British radio stations calling for bearings which put him somewhere near King's Lynn.

"At about this time he found a British ship, the collier *Franz Fischer*, anchored in the mouth of the Thames estuary. One of *Franz Fischer's* three survivors saw a bomb fall from the zeppelin, which was stationary above the ship. It entered the *Franz Fischer's* funnel, the explosion blew out the bottom and the unlucky vessel sank in less than a minute.

"The next report from *L-19* is its captain saying over the wireless: 'Radio equipment at times out of order. Three engines out of order. Approximate position Borkum Island.'

"Sentries in neutral Holland put *L-19* further south over Dutch territory. They had fired at the airship with everything they had until it disappeared out to sea."

A Grimsby steam trawler skipper, William Martin, said that before daybreak on February 2, he saw lights flashing in the distance. "I went towards the lights and discovered a huge mass of wreckage on the water," he told a correspondent from *The Times* newspaper. "I stood by and at daybreak found the wreckage was that of a large German airship bearing the identification mark *L-19*. The cabins were under water and so was a large part of the envelope, but a large portion was still above water.

"On a raised platform on top of the envelope were seven or eight members of the crew, who hailed us in broken English saying, 'Save us, save us! We will give you plenty of money.' One officer offered gold."

Skipper Martin of the unarmed trawler felt it would be unwise to take the zeppelin's men aboard, as they outnumbered his own crew. So he left the scene and reported the incident to a British naval vessel. As he sailed away the enemy was shouting, "Gott strafe England!"

Afterwards a gale came up. Despite a general search, the airship was never seen again; thus it probably foundered, taking all down with it.

This strange tale gives some idea of the exact position of the zeppelin, but a further amazing twist does tell us where Captain Loewe thought he was sinking. Six months after the trawler's encounter with the downed zeppelin, a bottle with a note in it washed ashore on the coast in Sweden. The message read: "With 15 men on the top platform and backbone girder of the L-19, floating without gondolas. I am attempting to send a last report. Engine trouble three times repeated, a light headwind on the return journey delayed our return and, in the mist, carried us over Holland where I was received with heavy rifle fire; the ship became heavy and simultaneously three engines failed. February 2, 1916, towards 1 p.m. will apparently be our last hour. – Loewe."

# 50

## *Bianca's double death*

The Boston vessel *Commonwealth*, a steam-powered tern schooner converted into a fresh fish trawler, arrived in Halifax on August 29, 1918, with the vessel *Bianca* in tow. Storm-tossed and damaged schooners, small traders, steamers and ocean liners limping into port or under tow was not an event that was especially noteworthy in one of North America's busiest seaports. But the marine misadventure and type of damage inflicted on the Shelburne-built *Bianca* was so unique that *The Halifax Herald* of August 30, 1918, said, "The arrival of the *Bianca* at this port was a complete surprise to shipping men and this morning hundreds of people visited Campbell and Company's wharf to look at the schooner."

The question uppermost on people's minds as they viewed *Bianca* had to be: What happened to its crew and what caused the damage to this fine schooner? The answer to the latter wasn't long coming. *Commonwealth*'s crew were sure a German raider had intercepted and captured *Bianca*, set a timed or fused bomb on it and left the vessel to sink.

Although the news was delayed in getting to shipping authorities in Halifax, the media soon learned the fate of *Bianca*'s crew. One day before the *Commonwealth* and its tow reached port, *Bianca*'s nine crewmen had rowed into Isaac's Harbour, a village located approximately 120 miles north-east of Halifax.

Owned by the Bowring Company of Newfoundland, the 313-ton *Bianca* was termed "an auxiliary vessel," for in addition to a great spread of canvas on its three masts, it was equipped with an engine. Captain Mark Burke of Car-bonear, Newfoundland, was hired to take *Bianca* to southern ports with a cargo of fish. Despite the danger to ships by the German war machine's all-out attempts to cripple foreign exports, sea trade to and from Europe continued across the North Atlantic. Many fine schooners and steamers fell prey; *Bianca* was one of the unlucky ones.

On August 25, while about a hundred miles east of Halifax, Burke was returning home with a full cargo of dry tobacco aboard *Bianca*, when his vessel was stopped by an enemy ship. Captain Burke and his crew (only one name has been recorded, thirty-year-old engineer J. Coady) were ordered into the schooner's lifeboat and told to leave the scene, for their vessel would be sunk.

It was the custom for the enemy to set a timed or fused bomb aboard the lonely and unarmed merchant schooners they captured. Expensive torpedoes were reserved for larger, more valuable targets. Captain Burke said that as they rowed away they did not hear an explosion, leading him to believe that one bomb had detonated. It could only be assumed that, rather than finishing *Bianca* off, the enemy chose to keep the derelict afloat as a decoy to trap other Allied ships.

Burke and his crew set a course for the Nova Scotian coast. Fortunately, the mid-August weather was settled, the ocean was relatively calm and they rowed into Isaac's Harbour on August 28.

The trawler *Commonwealth* had been out fishing. On Monday, August 26, it was ready to resume work on the Western Bank. After ten days of trawling, Captain Watts had 130,000 pounds of fish aboard. While moving to another fishing ground, it inadvertently located the erstwhile tern schooner *Bianca*.

One of *Commonwealth*'s crew said they were "about 110 miles east of Halifax when someone aboard saw a vessel about two miles off that was listing to one side." He reported: "Our captain, Frank Watts, gave the order to proceed to the aid of the derelict which, on examination, we found to be the *Bianca*, laden with a cargo of tobacco. The vessel was partly full of water while the sails were lying in the water on one side.

"A number of our crew were sent on board and found that the cabins had been rifled and all papers destroyed by the submarine crew. Letters and cabin furnishings were strewn about the deck, while a large bundle of the ship's papers were found floating in the water on the aft part of the deck. The papers were examined, but the writing was obliterated so badly that it was impossible to make it out.

"The only living thing found on *Bianca* was a small male pup which was dancing around in a playful mood when the crew went onboard."

*Commonwealth*'s crew could plainly see that the schooner was once handsomely furnished, but the enemy had smashed the fittings, furnishings and anything else moveable or fixed. Captain Watts and his crew tried to right the vessel, but a heavy gale came on and they had to abandon the work. They figured the vessel and cargo would be worth a fair share of salvage monies, a good dollar in addition to pay for fish

The *Halifax Herald* of August 30, 1918, has a photo of the *Bianca*, showing people at the dockside in Halifax admiring the strength and stability of the ship.

already on board. The next morning, when the wind died out, they succeeded in righting Bianca, repairing sails and clearing the deck. With the Bianca in tow, Commonwealth steered for Halifax.

Bianca was worth $50,000, not including the cargo. Captain Watts figured the German raiders took a good supply of tobacco and left the remainder to go to the bottom. Water, which swept the decks of Bianca as it lay on its side, worked its way into the hold and had ruined most of the cargo. Salvage liabilities, ship and cargo, plus the cost of towing, was tendered at $125,000.

Commonwealth's nineteen men were awarded one-third that amount; the local papers facetiously referred to the final payout as salvage monies worth "a small fortune." Most of the crew were from Boston, but two hailed from Nova Scotia: E. Mason from Lunenburg and Everett Thibeau of Yarmouth.

Bianca, even with part of its bottom pushed out from the explosion of the bomb, lay at a Halifax wharf seemingly as a tribute to the substantial handiwork and construction skills of Shelburne shipbuilders. According to veteran mariners, the shock of the explosion must have been considerable; nevertheless, its hull withstood the blast and "the strength of the materials is proof of good and true work put into building Bianca." When the cargo was removed, the tern went to the Halifax marine slip for permanent repairs.

The end of the staunch schooner Bianca is recorded in Frank Saunders' book Sailing Vessels and Crews of Carbonear. Once damages were repaired and salvage monies paid, Bowrings put Bianca back into the foreign trade. A little over one year after its near-death experience, Bianca sailed its last voyage with Mark Burke still in command. On October 21, 1919, it left Labrador for Portugal with salt fish. Three days later, in a heavy ocean swell, the engineer reported water over the kelson near the engine room and, on sounding for leaks in the fish hold, discovered three feet of water in that part of the doomed ship.

Immediately Burke ordered the engines stopped and the pumps manned. By October 28, the wind freshened and the well-laden *Bianca* wallowed in the troughs and crests of high swells. Burke ordered the cargo jettisoned and only after 1,200 quintals (about 135,000 pounds) were thrown over board did the schooner become a little more buoyant. At 8 a.m. the next morning a mountainous sea swept the deck and did the final damage, carrying away the main boom and tearing away the companion way leading to the engine room, flooding the engine room. On deck the rails were torn off and the two lifeboats were reduced to rubble.

Not long after, the S.S. *Lehigh*, commanded by Captain James Deal and bound for Charleston, South Carolina, sighted the sinking ship. *Bianca*'s lifeboats were broken up, so Deal lowered a lifeboat and his sailors rowed over to pluck nine weary Newfoundland sailors from a watery grave.

In his official statement of *Bianca*'s loss to the ship owners, Burke described the last moments: ". . . To our exhausted crew the *Lehigh* came like a gift of Providence. When the *Lehigh*'s boat came alongside our waterlogged vessel, orders were given for the crew to bring nothing with them but to jump for dear life to the lifeboat. On board kind hands directed my men to the crew's quarters where they were stripped of their sodden garments and clad in dry underwear. Falling into warm berths provided we were soon asleep. The traditions of the sea were nobly maintained by the master and the gallant crew of *Lehigh*."

# 51

## Wreckage: Mute evidence of disaster

September 1921

The message dated September 19, 1921, to Ritcey Brothers of Riverport, Nova Scotia, was traumatic. Although the brothers had been expecting bad news of the sinking or the wreck of their schooner *Otokio*, the heartrending information it contained was hard to take. The message stated that wreckage had been found on Sober Island off Beaver Harbour, Nova Scotia. It confirmed the worst possible fears – Captain Newton Ritcey and his crew of fifteen men were gone.

The *Otokio* and its fishermen had been missing since the night of a gale on Friday, September 6. Initial reports claim fifteen men were on the vessel, but according to the *Halifax Chronicle-Herald* of September 21, *Otokio* carried five dories, indicating ten dorymen plus three others who tended the vessel while the dories were fishing. This shows the vessel probably had thirteen crewmen.

The schooner left Port Hawksbury on the afternoon of September 6 and was in sight of other schooners until after dark.

REMAINS OF THE SHIP EUGENIE WRECKED AT BALLYMACOTTER
BAY, IRELAND

The wreckage in this image from the *Illustrated London News*, December 15, 1866, is comparable to debris from *Otokio* that drifted ashore in September 1921 at Beaver Harbour, Nova Scotia.

When the other vessels arrived, each with stories of hardship during the fiercest gale that swept the Nova Scotian eastern coast in fifty years, it was expected daily the *Otokio* would make port somewhere. But as each day went by with no word, a certain uneasiness began to appear among seagoing men, and the unspeakable words were in the minds of those around Riverport and Lunenburg: "*Otokio* has gone under."

Soon, unmistakable debris gave mute evidence to a major sea disaster. The bulwarks of a schooner washed ashore on the island. Nearby were oars marked with the initials W.R. and G.H., supposedly belonging to Wallace Ritcey and George Heisler. Today, *Otokio* is posted as "Lost with Crew."

# 52

## The women's tale: Shipwreck, fire, hard luck

December 1921

"You can imagine our fright," said May Oxner. "We were sitting in the cabin, when the first big sea swept over the boat. It splintered the skylight, which came crashing down on our heads."

Talk about tough luck. A wave smashing the skylight was only the beginning of a series of marine misadventures which ended with a fire (in a train baggage room) that destroyed the women's belongings.

On December 2, 1921, the schooner *Donald J. Cook*, a 101-ton two-master registered in Riverport, Nova Scotia, left St. John's bound for Jamaica. It carried its regular crew: Captain Percey Oxner, cook Bennett Taylor and four or five deck hands, probably all from Riverport or Lunenburg. But in addition, the *Donald J.* had two women aboard – the captain's wife, May Oxner, and Mrs. Taylor, the cook's wife. It started out as a pleasure trip for the ladies, although it was the dead of winter, a time of boisterous seas in the North Atlantic. They were bound for the West Indies' warmer climes and were, in the beginning, quite enthusiastic for a sea voyage with their husbands.

Hard luck began on the first day of the journey when the schooner ran into bad weather off Newfoundland. Five days later, still coasting down to Jamaica, the *Donald J.* was hit by a winter gale. One squall struck the schooner, carrying away its foresail, jumbo and jib. In the more intense storm which followed, tremendous seas continually swept over the vessel, wrecked the cabin and practically ruined the ship's store of food and supplies.

The wave that shattered the skylight partly filled the cabin with water where the two women were clinging to the table for support, waiting for some other news that the ship was in trouble. They rushed on deck to see what was happening and to get some reassurance from the sailors attempting to hold the *Donald J. Cook* on a steady keel.

May Oxner recalled, "We were both thoroughly frightened by that time and went up on deck to investigate. Here we found the men, working like mad to secure the mainsail which every sea threatened to sweep away. They struggled with it for quite a while, but the force of the waves was too great for them and the sea swept the sail overboard, taking with it the main boom and gaff.

"Left with no sail, we were at the mercy of the sea and drifted for five days. Luckily we had plenty of food on board, although it was badly damaged by the water. Water was very deep in the hold and waves continually washed over the ship."

It was during those days of drifting on a demented sea on an out-of-control ship that the crew and passengers prayed for help. Just as all hope was nearly abandoned, the lights of a vessel came in sight.

According to May Oxner, *Donald J. Cook*'s mainsail blew away on a Monday and it was not until the following Saturday night that the lights of a passing vessel appeared on the horizon. "Every light and flare aboard the *Donald J.* was brought out," she recalled – everything from a flashlight to cabin lamps. But the steamer evidently did not see the signals and continued on its course.

By then Captain Oxner knew his wallowing schooner was in serious trouble and fervently hoped and prayed for salvation for the sake of the frightened women, his beleaguered crew and himself. He ordered regular watches day and night, posting crew to scan for another ship. There was no sight of anything and hope that their lives would be spared began to fade. The crew was almost exhausted from the loss of sleep, the cold and a lack of proper food.

Sunday afternoon at 4 p.m. the outline of another steamer appeared in the distance – the S.S. *Sanduardo*, bound for Bermuda. It changed direction, steamed down to the struggling schooner and maneuvered close by. One of its officers came aboard the *Donald J. Cook* and said that the *Sanduardo* would tow them to Bermuda, the nearest port.

When they opened the hatches, Oxner and his crew discovered the schooner was leaking badly and water in the hold had risen several feet. Captain Oxner had no choice. The *Donald J.* was abandoned at latitude 30 degrees North, longitude 58.30 West. Two and a half hours later, just as the steamer was getting underway with the rescued safely aboard, the battered and waterlogged hulk went down. The men and women aboard the schooner had gotten off just in the nick of time.

# SURVIVORS OF THE DONALD J. COOK LOSE ALL THEIR BELONGINGS IN THE FIRE THAT RAZES LUNENBURG DEPOT

**Women Tell of Terrible Experiences on Board Schooner Lost in the Atlantic.**

Special to The Herald.

RIVERPORT, Feb. 8—The hard luck which pursued the members of the crew of the schooner Donald J. Cook, ran true to form up to the last stage of their journey home from Mexico.

Arriving in Lunenburg yesterday afternoon, Mrs. May Oxner, wife of the captain of the ill-fated schooner, and several other members of the crew, stored their belongings, saved from the schooner, when they were rescued, in the baggage room of the Lunenburg station, to await transportation to Riverport. At 9.30 that evening, fire which broke out in the station, completely destroyed their effects, which, it is stated, contained a number of valuable souvenirs of their exciting trip.

CAPT. PERCY OXNER

Captain Oxner under the headlines "Survivors . . . Lose All Belongings" on page three of *The Halifax Herald*, February 9, 1922.

The captain of the ship gave up his cabin to the two women and everything was done to ensure their personal comfort. "I have to say that the crew of *Sanduardo* treated us exceptionally well," said May Oxner.

But the loss of the *Donald J.* – May Oxner and Mrs. Taylor's vacation "home on the sea" – initiated a lengthy and unscheduled tour to southern lands. Twelve days after the crew and the two women were picked up by the *Sanduardo* they were carried first to Bermuda and then landed at Puerta, Mexico. There they stayed for eleven days, as the British Consul advised them not to take a train north, but to wait for a boat. The railway service was none too reliable in Mexico in that era and was subject to numerous accidents.

It was mid-January 1922 before they sailed by the *San Antonio* to Port Texas, thence by the S.S. *Elego* to New York. On February 2, the *Donald J.*'s travel-weary group left by train for Nova Scotia, arriving there six days later.

It seemed like the end of a long series of misadventures, but there was one more hardship to endure. The *Halifax Chronicle-Herald* reports:

Riverport, February 8

**Women Tell of Terrible Experience on Board Schooner.**

"The hard luck which pursued the members of the crew of the schooner *Donald J. Cook* ran true to form up the last stage of their journey home from Mexico.

"Arriving in Lunenburg yesterday afternoon, Mrs. May Oxner and several other members of the crew stored their belongings saved from the schooner when they were rescued. In their effects they also had a number of valuable souvenirs from Bermuda, Mexico and the United States. Belongings and souvenirs were in the baggage room of the Lunenburg train station to await transportation to Riverport.

"At 9:30 that evening fire broke out in the station and completely destroyed their baggage, clothes, souvenirs and other personal effects."

# 53

## *cA victim of the sands of Sable*

cAbout 150 miles east of Halifax lies a treacherous sandy reef known as Sable Island. Often shrouded in fog, Sable Island has been trapping and sinking ships for hundreds of years. Ships that strike the vise-like beaches there almost never get off. And many of them disappear in a short time beneath the ever-shifting sand.

Because of its many shipwrecks, Sable Island is known – like many other wreck-strewn areas on the coast of the North Atlantic – as the "Graveyard of the Atlantic." Since the 1500s there have been more than 350 recorded ship-wrecks on the shores of the island.

There is a map of Sable Island shipwrecks produced by the Nova Scotia Department of Education, showing the location and year of many wrecks. Each point or dot with its ship's name listed on the map has a story. However, many names on the map, their crews and destinations are now lost in time; their ocean odysseys and hardships near Sable Island are unknown or, at the very best, obscure.

One wreck – although lacking a crew list and details of survival – has recently come to light. There on the shipwreck map squeezed in between the wreck of *Crofton Hall*, 1898, and *Malta*, 1869, is the tiny dot on the east side, marking where the *Harold Caspar* ended its career in 1926.

On February 24, 1926, the crew of the latest casualty of Sable Island, the British steamer *Harold Caspar*, arrived in Halifax on board the government steamer *Lady Laurier*. Asked about his experience on Sable Island, Captain Darkins said nothing except, "My ship struck Sable Island and is a total loss."

A ship of 1,865 tons, the *Harold Caspar* left England with five thousand tons of coal destined for New York. At 7 a.m. on Thursday, February 11, 1926, it hit the northwestern bar about a mile from shore, directly off the island's East Light. Captain Darkins knew his ship was stuck fast in the dreaded "Graveyard" and was not likely to come off soon. After two hours the twenty-eight crewmen prepared to leave the ship in their own boats. It was so foggy, Darkins and company didn't expect help from the island lifesaving crews.

As *Harold Caspar* began to break in two, the crew gathered up personal belongings, the captain collected his chronometer, log and other documents and they launched the lifeboats. The first people to meet the shipwrecked crew were the wireless operator and another man who had come down to the beach when the lifeboats neared the shore.

On Sunday, three days after *Harold Caspar* stranded, Captain Darkins, Chief Officer Busby and Engineer Geiple went out to the ship in a lifeboat. With a heavy load of coal aboard, the ship settled quickly in the soft sands.

Upon discovery of the wreck, Sable Island's wireless operator contacted shipping agencies in Halifax, but it was thirteen days before the S.S. *Lady Laurier* arrived to take off the marooned sailors. By the time *Lady Laurier* left the island, only a small part of *Harold Caspar*'s upper works was showing above the water and sand – the funnel was gone and one of the two spars had also disappeared.

# 54

## Baltic's encounter with a whale

September 1927

In its heyday, the passenger liner *Baltic II*, commonly referred to as *Baltic*, was considered one of the "Big Four" White Star liners along with *Celtic II*, *Cedric* and *Adriatic*. Sister ships to the *Titantic*, in pre-*Titanic* years, they were considered safe and reliable. Launched in 1903, the 24,000-ton *Baltic* made regular runs across the Atlantic until 1932 when it was scrapped. During World War I *Baltic* was engaged, like her sisters, in transporting troops, and after the war, she continued on the familiar route between Liverpool and New York.

But if regular and safe voyages were the norm, sometimes *Baltic*'s passengers were exposed to the unusual. On January 23, 1909, the *Florida* rammed White Star's passenger liner *Republic* in fog. Efforts to save *Republic* with improvised collision mats were not successful, and it eventually sank more than forty hours after the collision.

However, her Marconi radio operator, Jack Binns, managed to put out a call for assistance on the shattered remains of his radio equipment. The *Baltic* answered, appeared on the scene twelve hours after the collision, around 7:30 p.m., and took aboard all of *Republic*'s passengers within the next four hours. *Baltic* then began the rescue of the *Florida*'s passengers and crew, taking aboard 1,650 people and carrying them to port.

On one occasion in 1929, *Baltic* rescued the crew of the Newfoundland schooner *Northern Light*, sailing (or rather attempting to sail) from St. John's to Newtown, Bonavista Bay. A December storm blew her into the Atlantic and battered *Northern Light* into submission. On December 6, *Baltic*'s Captain Davis saw the wallowing ship and sent out a lifeboat crew to take off Captain Thomas Parsons and four members of his crew. One person on *Northern Light*, the captain's son, Rex Parsons of Newtown, drowned during the transfer and rescue.

Two years previous to this incident, in early September 1927, *Baltic* was steaming westward off the south coast of Ireland when it struck an eighteen-foot whale. The ship stopped and its seamen could see the whale was impaled on the liner's bow. When *Baltic* reversed, the whale floated free but a deep wound could be seen in its neck.

*Baltic*'s captain recalled other incidents between whales and ships, saying that whales were not always the victims; sometimes they attacked ships. The destroyer *Lamson* had been recently butted by a whale off the coast of Maine. The mammal, a fairly large one, seemed to take offense with the vessel and turned on it. *Lamson*'s engines were reversed, but even so the shock of the impact made the whole ship tremble. It flung men out of their bunks and threw dishes out of the racks in the galley, smashing them. No serious harm was done and the whale dived and vanished.

A postcard of White Star's liner *Baltic*, a passenger ship involved in several adventures on the North Atlantic.

The whaler *Dimon*, while working near the Farœe Islands, was charged by a great whale with such force that its whole bow caved in. Water filled the forecastle and engine room, stopping the engines. The steam trawler *Salvia* came by, took off the crew of nine and the derelict was towed into port.

*Baltic's* captain said, "One of the most famous cases of whale-ship wrecks I know of happened between one of the big old-fashioned whalers and a particularly large monster of the deep. *Essex* was into a school of sperm whales and its boats were busy harpooning and bringing in kills.

"A monstrous bull whale, the leader of a pod or herd, drew off some distance and rushed toward *Essex*. The men at the wheel saw what was happening, but that day the wind was light and the sailing ship could not be moved in time. The whale, which weighed at least eighty tons, crashed into the ship's side with such fury as to stave in thick planking.

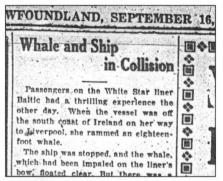

**WFOUNDLAND, SEPTEMBER 16,**

## Whale and Ship in Collision

Passengers on the White Star liner Baltic had a thrilling experience the other day. When the vessel was off the south coast of Ireland on her way to Liverpool, she rammed an eighteen-foot whale.

The ship was stopped, and the whale, which had been impaled on the liner's bow, floated clear. But there was a

The St. John's, Newfoundland, *Evening Telegram* of September 16, 1927, reports on an ill-fated encounter with a whale.

"Not content, the great beast charged a second time, and this finished the *Essex*. It sank in less than half an hour, and its crew barely had enough time to launch the small boats and row away."

According to Robert F. Burgess' book *Sinkings, Salvages, and Shipwrecks* (1970), *Essex*'s boats became separated and were repeatedly attacked by sharks. When their meagre food supplies ran out, the starving men were reduced to cannibalism. Three survivors were picked up by the English brig *India*. Then three months later, the skipper, Captain Pollard, and a crew member were found more dead than alive by the whaling ship *Dauphin*.

# 55

## The Belgian steamer and the Boston banker

*February 1932*

When the collision occurred, seas lashed by the gale, snow and flying spray shut out a clear view ahead. Captain Lavigne of the *Jean Jadot* said afterwards he had a good view of the little fishing schooner once, when he was about two and a half miles away. Then rolling waves and snow flurries blotted out his view of the other vessel.

When the rolling schooner next appeared, it loomed suddenly out of the greyness, hard under the *Jadot's* prow. The big liner could not respond properly, the captain said, to her hard down helm. The wind was sweeping her on, and the propeller was threshing sometimes in the water, sometimes out.

Bound west to New York, *Jean Jadot*, a steel-hulled passenger/freight liner of the Lloyd Royal Beige Line, left Antwerp on January 27, 1932. Although in an area frequented by fishing vessels, it steamed full ahead. By February 6, it was eighty miles off Cape Sable, Nova Scotia. It was 6:45 a.m. when the crash came.

On the schooner *Eleanor Nickerson*, only a few men were on deck. Most of the crew were below in cabins when the steel prow slashed into the wooden hull. *Eleanor Nickerson* had twenty-seven fishermen aboard, mostly from Nova Scotia, the rest from the Boston area.

*Eleanor Nickerson* had left Boston on February 1, for the fishing banks east of LaHave, Nova Scotia. Built in Essex in 1927 and valued at $60,000, the 110-foot-long schooner had an auxiliary motor capable of maintaining eight miles an hour. On the morning of February 6, however, it lay to, anchored for the night. Most of the crew were asleep in their bunks.

Upon impact, someone on *Nickerson*'s deck cut the lashing from a nest of dories. Five men managed to lower themselves into one, only to find the drain hole at the bottom was not plugged and the plug was missing. They quickly transferred to another dory. Meanwhile, the schooner, fatally cut through, was going down. No one below deck made it topside. A sixth man, Frank LeBlanc, struggled in the water. He was trying to kick off his heavy boots when a high wave washed him into the boat with the other five.

The *Jean Jadot* slowed down after impact, slowly swinging around to see the damage done. Captain Lavigne said when the schooner suddenly appeared, hard under the steamer's prow, his larger liner could not change direction quickly enough to avoid collision.

The six survivors of *Eleanor Nickerson* somehow managed to get to the side of the steamer where they were pulled aboard. Surviving were Frank and Mark LeBlanc, Calvin Hemeon, Edmund Burbine, Arthur Burke and Patrick Feltmate, the latter from Nova Scotia.

On Friday noon, February 6, Captain Lavigne wired this message to the nearest American Coast Guard station: "Collided and sank this morning fishing schooner *Eleanor Nickerson* of Boston at position 43.05 North and 63.45 West. Rescued six members of crew, twenty-one missing. Expect arrive quarantine Saturday evening."

The Coast Guard then instructed all patrol boats near the position given to be on the lookout for wreckage and to make a thorough search should any be found. *Nickerson's* owner in Boston, Arthur L. Parker, thought that no dory filled with men could have survived the blizzard raging at the time of the wreck. Lavigne also wired the Halifax agent of the Department of Marine to request all ships in the vicinity of the wreck to stand by and keep a watch for survivors.

It was not to be. There were no other survivors. Captain Irving Morrissey, of Lower East Pubnico, Nova Scotia, and twenty men had gone down with the schooner *Eleanor Nickerson*.

The great loss of life and wreck of a valuable schooner should have taught the owners and captain of the liner a lesson, but five years later, in July 1937, history repeated itself. The *Jean Jadot* again rammed a fishing schooner anchored on the Banks. The *Pauline Lohnes* carried twenty-three men; this time, though, the crew was not below and asleep. Twenty were out in dories hauling trawls on the fishing grounds.

In the evening fog of July 17, Captain Augot of the *Pauline Lohnes* heard the ominous shriek of a steam whistle. Unable to see any approaching vessel, he immediately ordered the schooner's fog horn to sound continuously as a warning to his dorymen and perhaps to signal the onrushing ship.

A few moments after, the captain saw a large steamer bearing directly down on his schooner, and he commenced firing the swivel, a small cannon used to signal dorymen. Both signals proved useless in alerting the charging ship, which evidently did not see the schooner.

Had *Jean Jadot* struck at night when most of the crew would have been asleep in the forecastle, the impact would have meant instant death for many. Within five minutes the Newfoundland schooner sank, going down headfirst. Two of her dories arrived from tending fishing gear, no doubt attracted by the foghorn and swivel gun, in time to see the whole spectacle. The last three of the schooner's dories pulled up later quite surprised to see, where their home base should be, a large Belgian steamer. The fishermen were all picked up without mishap and carried to New York. From there they were transported home.

Twice in five years the Belgian steamer rammed and sank fishing schooners – the first with many fatalities – the second with none.

# 56

## Rumrunner turned pirate

*December 1933*

On December 7, 1933, ships in the North Atlantic picked
up a strange wireless radio message from the Marconi station at Glace Bay, Nova Scotia: "The rumrunner motor vessel
*Kromhout*, 125 feet long, was seized by patrol *Cutter No. 4* last
night. During the night the *Kromhout* cut the tow line and
escaped. It is requested that you keep a lookout for this vessel
and wire all details to the R.C.M.P. at Sydney or at Glace
Bay."

The odd missive indicated a rumrunner had broken cus-
tody, the captain and crew were fugitives on the ocean and
that a chase, a game of hide and seek on the high seas, was in
progress. What happened next came out when two pieces of
evidence were presented weeks later: the log of the R.C.M.P.
*Cutter No. 4* and the testimony of *Kromhout*'s Captain Mason.

The schooner *Kromhout*. (John Kingwell, Knickle's Studio and Gallery, Dartmouth, Nova Scotia)

The cutter plowed the storm-tossed seas off Louisbourg Fairway Buoy before daylight on December 6. Through the gale and howling winds, Captain Moyle Hyson heard the bow lookout shout that there was something off the port bow. He could only tell through the dark and sleet because he heard "five bells" strike, indicating another ship nearby was changing watch. Hyson ordered out the searchlights. Ordinarily, the cutter may not have intercepted a lonely ship, but this one was running without lights. The searchlight stopped on a ship far to port, a tossing shadow and a reflection on the strange ship's glass or brass.

Sailing without lights and apparently heading from St. Pierre toward Lunenburg meant the mystery ship was probably carrying a load of contraband rum. Officers on *Cutter No. 4* studied the vessel through binoculars and saw its lines: long and rakish, fore and aft masts with a rag of a foresail up.

> ### Crew of *Kromhout,*
> ### December 1933
>
> Capt. Ross Mason, Louisbourg
>
> Mate, Fred Acker, Louisbourg
>
> Arthur Knickle, Lunenburg
>
> Lorrain Mason, Lunenburg
>
> Wallace Greek, Lunenburg
>
> Fred Tanner, Lunenburg
>
> Wilbert Greek, Lunenburg
>
> Jessen Morash, Lunenburg

It was the wooden auxiliary (powered by either wind or by motor) schooner *Kromhout*, a renowned and illusive rumrunner. Captain Hyson consulted his reports to verify that *Kromhout* was on the wanted list. It had been apprehended ten months previously as it landed contraband near Louisbourg.

If the *Kromhout* was outside the twelve-mile Canadian territorial limit, its crew could not be arrested, but charts and bearings told Captain Hyson *Kromhout* was inside that limit, less than ten miles from the coast. The crew uncovered a little four-pound cannon in the bow of *Cutter No. 4* and fired a few warning shots at the rumrunner.

*Kromhout* slowed down. Hyson put off the dory with a boarding crew. However, when they came near they could see the smuggler's captain shaking his fist as if to say, 'No one's coming aboard this schooner.' With that dire warning, *Kromhout* got under way again.

After picking up his dory crew, Hyson gave chase, saying, "When we get close, put a warning shot across the bow and if that doesn't work, put a live one in its hull."

When Captain Mason saw the white water where the first warning shot hit the sea, he stopped. This time the cutter's prize crew, Chief Officer Milton MacKenzie, engineer James McIntosh, seamen Raymond Oxford and Murdock McDonald, all of Cape Breton, boarded the fugitive. *Kromhout* did have contraband, more than 1,500 cases of prime whiskey from St. Pierre.

Usually this would have ended a tale of hunt and find on the ocean, but it was only the beginning. The logbook of *Cutter No. 4* says that before the law officers took *Kromhout* in tow, Mason and his crew retreated to the engine room and bolted the door. Mason is alleged to have said, "Go ahead and break in. You got the ship, now tow it in."

Hyson's plan would have been for *Kromhout's* crew to do the sailing while under guard of the Mounties. Official records show that the mountainous seas made it impossible for Captain Hyson to put more men aboard the smuggler – one group to navigate *Kromhout* while another group overpowered Mason and his crew.

Neither vessel could come close without great danger of one smashing into the other. The stubborn craft would have to be towed. It pitched and ploughed and dragged at the end of ninety fathoms (540 feet) of hawser as the small cutter valiantly struggled toward Sydney, Nova Scotia.

Late in the night MacKenzie, at the *Kromhout's* wheel, felt the barrel of a gun against his back. It was Mason and he was under the influence of smuggled whisky. Another man was with him, pointing a gun at the second R.C.M.P. officer. MacKenzie spoke: "You know this is piracy."

"Piracy, be damned," said Mason. "This is my ship and I'm not going to let any . . . police take it away from me."

The newspapers of early December 1933 caught the public's attention with tales of rumrunning, smuggling, piracy, and hijacking. Yet within a few days, December 11, the honest hardworking sailors were freed. Subsequently, only the captain was "convicted of the theft of *Kromhout*" – his own ship.

MacKenzie surrendered. One of Mason's men went forward and cut the hawser. At that moment the remaining crew on *Cutter No. 4* were thrown forward from the release of the heavy tow behind them. Hyson went to the stern to see the lights of *Kromhout* wink and disappear as it drifted away behind the cutter. The line, he thought, had been cut or had snapped. He ordered the cutter turned around to give chase.

Meanwhile aboard the rumrunner, MacKenzie slipped away and hid from his adversaries, hoping to get a signal to the cutter. He would have been found, but Mason said to his crew, "Never mind him. We'll be in Miquelon in a few hours" – the tiny French island, north of St. Pierre. Mason and his crew had all they could do to keep an eye on the other captured police officer and to keep the ship stable in the storm.

MacKenzie was able to find a lantern and signal without *Kromhout*'s crew seeing him. Using his cap, he signaled by the dots and dashes of Morse code: "Mason takes ship prisoner. Headed Miquelon." He barely had the message complete when

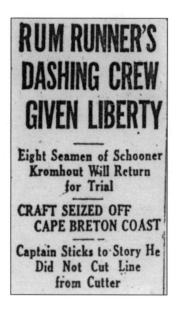

# RUM RUNNER'S DASHING CREW GIVEN LIBERTY

**Eight Seamen of Schooner Kromhout Will Return for Trial**

**CRAFT SEIZED OFF CAPE BRETON COAST**

**Captain Sticks to Story He Did Not Cut Line from Cutter**

## SHIP WAS DRIVING ON CAPE BRETON COAST

**Capt. Ross Mason Declares Action Saved His Craft from Disaster**

S. PIERRE, Dec. 9—The motorship Kromhout's dramatic dash seaward with four men of their captor patrol boat aboard was described by her skipper last night as an emergency measure that saved his liquor-laden craft from destruction in a storm driving her towards the Cape Breton coast.

From the St. Pierre jail where he and his crew were being detained Capt. Ross Mason sent word to the Kromhout's home port of Lunen-

The *Sydney Post-Record* of December 9 and 11, 1933, gives the rumrunning *Kromhout* front page status. Captain Ross Mason stated that his "action was only carried out to save his ship from disaster on the Cape Breton coast."

a bullet shattered the lantern and several of *Kromhout's* crew threw him to the deck.

But Captain Hyson had seen the furtive message and knew enough not to aggravate the enraged Mason in a futile chase. He set a course for Sydney. The wireless operator on *Cutter No. 4* had already flashed word of *Kromhout's* escape, asking ships in the area to keep a lookout for the renegade ship with its cargo of contraband and captured R.C.M.P. officers.

A more detailed message went to the head R.C.M.P. Inspector at Sydney. There, plans were put in place to capture the runaway ship. After all, it couldn't sail the ocean forever; it had to put in somewhere. Miquelon was its probable destination.

When *Kromhout*'s crew landed at the French islands of St. Pierre and Miquelon, about nine miles south of Newfoundland, a delegation waited for them. The prisoners were set free; Mason and crew were apprehended and held for deportation to Canada. Eventually, *Kromhout*'s seven seamen were released under an amicable settlement.

In the subsequent trial, only Captain Mason was convicted of the theft of *Kromhout* and its cargo, as well as obstructing police officers in the line of duty. He was given three years in prison – a relatively light sentence considering the serious list of crimes against him, but he stuck to his story – a valid explanation – that the tow line was not cut, but probably snapped in the storm. According to Mason in the *Sydney Post-Record* of December 11, 1933, "The *Kromhout* had been headed for the open sea to avoid being driven on the Cape Breton coast by heavy seas."

Captain Mason passed away in 1981 at Mason's Beach, Nova Scotia. He could never understand how any court could convict him of stealing his own ship.

As for the Lunenburg-built *Kromhout*, it was purchased in the 1940s by the Churchill family of Bay Roberts, Newfoundland, and used in the Labrador fishery. Later it went into the coastal trade. Around 1968, it was considered unfit for further use and was tied up in Trinity harbour, Newfoundland, where it later sank. A humiliating end for a Nova Scotian fishing vessel turned rumrunner, one involved with a high seas pursuit and a potentially dangerous capture of R.C.M.P. officers.

# 57

## A derelict, but which ship?

February 1934

While steaming eastward south of Cape Sable, Nova Scotia, on February 13, 1934, the Norwegian steamer *Taurus* passed a half-submerged derelict. It was obvious the vessel had been capsized by a storm and its crew probably drowned. Shipping authorities on Canada's east coast could only guess at its identity.

*Taurus*'s captain reported to the Department of Marine station at Yarmouth that swelling seas obscured the nameplate of the derelict. The crew saw no marks of identification, although the wreck was most likely a schooner. In the blinding snowstorm and high seas there was no chance to investigate the mystery ship off Nova Scotia. Through a swirl of snow a dark form, low in the water, appeared briefly and slipped silently past the steamer to disappear into the blackness astern.

The captain's message stated: "Passed what seems to be wrecked schooner bottom up about twenty miles south of Cape Sable. No identifying marks. Thick snow."

The Yarmouth station sent the message out to other shipping agencies along the coast, warning them to be on the lookout for a derelict, a menace to navigation. At this time three ships were missing or had not been heard from for some time; thus any of those three was the possible identity of the unknown derelict.

The first and most likely vessel was Lunenburg's *Agnes J. Myra*. The last heard from this schooner was a wireless message giving its position off Cape Breton just prior to a storm in late fall of 1933. The little schooner yacht *Osipee*, overdue to Bermuda, carried a group of Ontario sailors. A slim possibility existed that the derelict was the Nova Scotian iron-hulled schooner *Dorin*, missing for months.

On February 14, the Canadian government steamer *Arras* prepared to cruise the waters off Cape Sable. Before *Arras* left, its captain, Clement Barkhouse, declined to pinpoint which vessel he thought it might be, but said it was not likely the little *Osipee*. The thirteen-ton *Osipee*, officially given up on January 30, 1934, left Lunenburg early that month for Bermuda. By February it would have been far off the coast and closer to Bermuda.

Captain Angus Walters of the famed fishing and racing schooner *Bluenose* expressed his opinion on *Osipee*, a vessel he had helped outfit in Lunenburg. Walters pointed out that the weather had been fine for the first few days after the vessel left, and that meant it had probably reached waters much further south. *Osipee* carried three young people from Ontario: G. Batson of Brantford and Henry Labatt and George Keller, both from Hamilton. Walters believed that the young men had missed Bermuda and had probably sailed on into a southern port in the United States.

According to news re-ports of February 1934, *Agnes J. Myra*, built in Smith and Rhuland Shipyards, Lunenburg, in 1926, carried a crew of nine – this was subsequently revised to seven. This ship had reached the Cape Breton coast in October 1933 after a voyage to the West Indies. The last message from the schooner said it was awaiting favourable weather for a run south into Lunenburg.

> ### Crew of the missing *Agnes J. Myra*
>
> Isaiah Conrad, LaHave
>
> William Hubley, Lunenburg
>
> Doyle Robert Knickle, Garden Lots, 49, married, 2 children
>
> Leo Gustavus Sampson, Lunenburg, married
>
> Clarence Theodore "Ted" Tancook, Mahone Bay, 26, single
>
> George William Harris Tanner, Stonehurst, 50, married
>
> Norman Carson, Newfoundland

The next day a storm swept the Atlantic seaboard. After that, there was only an ominous silence from *Agnes J. Myra*.

The *Dorin* disappeared about the same time as the *Myra*. It had sailed from Nova Scotia for the Bahamas and left Turks Island laden with salt for the run north. It stopped at Nassau for fuel and, after heading out of the harbour there, vanished. A few days after *Dorin* sailed north, a series of hurricanes whipped the United States coast. Owner J.T. Cruickshank of Halifax believed these pounded the vessel and it foundered in the storm. His brother, age twenty-two and the ship's second engineer, was making his first voyage on *Dorin*.

While landsmen speculated on the identity of the wreck, the prospect of bad weather meant delays in the search. Government icebreakers were at work from Cape Breton to Yarmouth clearing harbours of drift ice that had prevented several ships from getting to or from port.

The derelict was never located after that initial sighting by *Taurus*. Eventually, the *Osipee*, *Agnes J. Myra* and *Dorin* remained unreported and today are listed in North American shipping registries as "Missing with Crew."

# 58

## The peculiar voyage of the Faröese

September 1935

In the recorded – that is, written – accounts, as well in the folklore or anecdotal tales of ships and wrecks on the North American side of the great Atlantic, there are many stories of ships being blown eastward across the Atlantic. The prevailing winds in winter pushed many a sail-driven schooner from Nova Scotia, Newfoundland and New England out into the Atlantic and far from home. Many tales are spun of ships that ended up in Scotland, or off the west coast of Ireland or England when in actual fact they were trying to get from Nova Scotia to Massachusetts or from Newfoundland to Nova Scotia.

But rare are the stories of European sail-driven vessels being pushed westward against their will and despite the opposite intentions of crew. In September 1935, the wooden vessel *Coronet* from the Faröe Islands ended up in Newfoundland, much to the surprise of the crew. Seventy-seven feet long and with a displacement of sixty tons, Coronet was built in Grimbsy, England, in 1887. The twenty-one-man crew were all from the Farðe Islands; none could speak a word of English.

In early September 1935 it left Greenland for the Farðe Islands (seventeen Danish-owned islands) located about 850 miles from Denmark. It was well-laden with a cargo of salted cod. A storm came on – as it so often does in any month on the hungry North Atlantic – and, although the vessel had a small engine, all its extra fuel, stored in drums on deck, was swept overboard in the storm.

On September 7, the badly buffeted Coronet was storm damaged and drifting westward. Captain Jenson decided to cut the engine to save the remaining fuel in case it would be needed to get the ship to harbour or shelter, if they ever found any in eastern North America. He knew the current and winds would take him southerly to Newfoundland or, if he missed the great island, perhaps somewhere southwest to Nova Scotia, New England – who knew where? And would he find help and habitation when the ship finally sighted land?

A subsequent report of conditions aboard Coronet as it drifted helplessly recounts the voyage: "The first heavy sea broke off the foremast to the deck. Then the bowsprit was smashed off. The wheelhouse was swept overboard, taking all nautical instruments with it and a little later all the boats were washed away.

"The vessel drifted helplessly before the fury of the sea and without an instrument it was impossible to get a bearing. Considerable water found its way into the engine room. The men had a narrow escape from being washed overboard several times while working the pumps.

"Captain Jenson said that it was a miracle to him that the vessel did not run ashore in the treacherous waters. The vessel had about two hundred quintals [about 23,000 pounds] of fish aboard as some of the cargo had been jettisoned during the storm."

On September 20, the crew saw a lighthouse, the Cabot Island light off Newfoundland's northwestern coast, but they didn't know where or what light it was. That morning the Knee family fishermen – George, Harry, Chesley and young Baxter Knee – were out on the fishing grounds off Flower's Island, near Cabot Island. They saw a vessel with no wheelhouse, rigging, masts – a derelict – and knew it was in trouble. They went alongside, but no one aboard could speak English and the Knees couldn't speak Danish. Harry Knee got aboard and Captain Jenson indicated by signs the motor wasn't working and they wished to be towed or piloted to a harbour.

The Newfoundland fishermen directed them to a pier in Valleyfield. There was perhaps no one within miles and miles of coastline who could speak any foreign language, let alone Danish. But there was one exception. A Mrs. Oakley from nearby Wesleyville, while in the United States, had married a Swede named Karl Anderson who could adequately converse in all Scandinavian languages. Mr. and Mrs. Anderson had recently moved to Wesleyville.

Soon the story of the twenty-one castaways was known all over Newfoundland's northeast coast. The Faröese, extremely grateful someone had guided them to safety, were given a passage to St. John's. The Newfoundland fishermen thought nothing of it, as a tow or help extended to distressed fishermen was a way of life they knew well and they expected no reward or remuneration.

Soon the crew was en route home to the Faröe Islands, but the storm-damaged *Coronet* stayed behind. The Crosbies of St. John's purchased the vessel, repaired it and put it under the command of Captain Abe Winsor of Wesleyville. *Coronet*, renamed *Hazel Pearl* after Winsor's two daughters, was used in the local fishery. It struck ice in Champney's West, Newfoundland, and sank on February 28, 1945 – nearly ten years after its serendipitous arrival in Newfoundland.

Although the story of the unexpected visit of *Coronet* remained part of the folktales of the people of Valleyfield and Wesleyville, the local fishermen went on with their fishery and lives. To their surprise in 1998, sixty-three years after the *Coronet*'s epic voyage, a man from the Faröe Islands contacted Baxter Knee. At the time of the rescue, Baxter was a boy of nine helping his father. He was the only one of the crew still alive from that September day in 1935.

As part of Denmark's National Remembrance Day celebrations, a video production crew made a documentary of *Coronet*'s voyage. Paul Kunoy, the son of *Coronet*'s first mate, came to northeastern Newfoundland. Thus in July 2000 when the epic was recreated, the people of the Faröe Islands and Newfoundland were again reunited in an age-old tale of the sea.

# 59

## Short interview for a long time adrift

*November 1946*

The towboat *Glenfield* had three tugs – each manned by one sailor – behind it when heavy seas forced the skipper to abandon one tug, knowing he was also setting it adrift with someone aboard. He had no choice; not to let it go adrift would probably mean all four vessels would be swallowed by an angry ocean.

Early in November 1946, workmen at Lunenburg's Smith and Rhuland yards finished attaching three tugs to *Glenfield*. Supplied with a good store of food and water, the tugs were being delivered to Liverpool for outfitting. Apart from food, water and some fuel, there was little else aboard.

The last tug in the line was the *Tanac*, seventy feet long and one of several tugs completed in the Lunenburg yards from late 1945 to 1946 – *Tanac-V-262* through to the *V-265*. At sea one of the *Tanacs* was manned by twenty-two-year-old

Kenneth Lohnes of Riverport, Nova Scotia. That's all that was needed: one deckhand; there was no seamanship or maintenance involved. It was easy work, a slow voyage to Liverpool that should have lasted just several hours.

On November 5 an intense storm broke as *Glenfield* steamed slowly southward. In the wind and high seas the tow line broke and all three vessels drifted away. The *Glenfield* recovered two tugs but heavy seas forced it to abandon the third.

A search by sea and air began immediately. For one week thousands of square miles of sea were covered, but there was no sign of *Tanac* or its sole occupant. Finally, heavy weather, cloud cover and limited visibility forced officials to call off the search. All coastal vessels plying the waters off southern Nova Scotia were asked to keep a lookout for the drifting vessel.

Soon old seamen and veteran mariners became skeptical. Wizened sea dogs doubted if *Tanac* could be found. Each passing day meant a small tug on the vast grey expanse of the North Atlantic would be harder to locate. It had no electronic equipment installed, so Lohnes was unable to signal his position or radio for help.

"I lost track of time," Lohnes said, "but I sure never lost interest in living and surviving." He saw no signs of searchers and although there was plenty of food aboard, the young man didn't feel like eating. Either there was no stove or Ken Lohnes didn't feel like lighting it. Cold beans, cold tinned soup, bread, biscuits didn't appeal to him as he kept a lonely vigil in a tossing moody Atlantic under black skies.

Never seasick a day in his life, Ken Lohnes was an excellent seaman and had already, in his youthful years, obtained his mate's ticket. In the high winds he stood before the wheel, kept *Tanac*'s head into the wind and tried to snatch a few moments sleep whenever he could. He said, "About three days ago I got the engine running and kept it going for about four hours, but I ran out of fuel. Then I dropped my anchors but the hawsers both parted and I danced along like a cork. When the weather got heavy I stayed at the wheel and ran before the winds. The only thing that bothered me was the thought that the people back home in Riverport would be worrying about me. I never thought I would be lost and I kept looking each morning for a sign of help."

In ten days of drifting he saw no sign of an airplane or ship; however, on two occasions he thought he heard the distant roar of airplane engines, but saw nothing flying overhead.

Then it happened. Something hove into sight. "Sure enough," said Lohnes, "this morning [November 15] I saw the Yankee Coast Guard bearing down on me. I said to myself, Ken, you're a lucky man. You're going home soon and have a hot meal."

The first thing he asked when the U.S. Coast Guard cutter *Pontchartrain* picked him up at 9:45 a.m. was "What day of the week is it?" He was also told he and the drifting *Tanac* were situated forty miles south of Cape Sable Island off the southern tip of Nova Scotia. Lohnes had a rough idea of where he was when found, but had "No idea of where I would end up if I wasn't picked up soon."

*Pontchartrain*, which found Lohnes three days after the organized search was called off, towed *Tanac* to the entrance of Shelburne harbour. From there the War Assets Corporation brought *Tanac* into Shelburne, where officials greeted the erstwhile mariner and wished to talk to him about the hazardous voyage.

Concerned people wanted to know if he felt okay and if his physical health and mental well-being had suffered. After all, they reasoned, ten days of cold and miserable drifting on a treacherous sea with no human companionship had to be nerve-wracking. He was asked how he felt. With a nonchalant shrug the seaman grinned and, using a Lunenburg expression, replied, "The finest kind! I'm going to make this interview short because I'm pretty darned hungry. I dropped forty pounds in weight in ten days which is why I feel like eating right now."

"When will you go to sea again?" asked the reporter.

"Well, mister, I'll tell you. Sometime in the middle of summer when the sea is smooth and there are plenty of hams aboard with me. And, I'll never travel alone again."

# 60

## *A tale both heroic and pathetic*

*September 1947*

The Newfoundland tern schooner *Harold* under Captain William Yetman was returning home to Harbour Grace just before New Year's Eve, 1904. Before it reached there, however, its story became not just a regional tale of its home port, Harbour Grace, but one shared with the great nation of Germany and a curious interaction of two towns.

Yetman and his five seamen had landed salt cod at Malaga, Spain, loaded salt at Cadiz for ballast and sailed west on December 2. On the third day out, the wind swung south southeast, very strong, and by December 5, the bad weather changed for the worse. Southeast gales turned to northwest with snow.

*Harold* iced up and had to run for warmer waters to help get the ice off the vessel. Yetman was determined to get home before Christmas; thus the next day his crew swung northerly again. They were doing well until December 18 when the winds came up, stronger than before.

Although the sails were reefed and the vessel lay to to ride out the storm, waves boarded the deck every minute. Yetman figured the winds were up to 95 mph with heavy rain and sometimes snow squalls. It was impossible to stand on deck without lifelines. A rogue wave, what seamen call an especially large one, broke over *Harold*, while the crew took shelter below.

Yetman took stock. Fortunately, no one was swept overboard, but the sight when the crew went on deck was best described as "devastation": the three masts, as well as the bowsprit, were broken off or damaged severely. Of the two anchors forward, one was gone overboard, the other had broken through the deck. The large lifeboat was missing, four casks of drinking water were smashed and the stove and furniture in the cabin were broken.

The crew was now without water, the fire in the damaged stove was out and they worked at getting canvas over the damaged section of the deck. By this time all hands had lifelines on, but when they saw a wave about to break over the ship, they all ran aft to take shelter in a companionway.

The pumps had to be kept going constantly. For fifteen days each man rotated for a fifteen minute turn pumping. The salt in the hold was melting and its brine was pumped out, but the crew could not keep against the inflow of water. On the fifteenth day, *Harold* was nearly full of water. All the nourishment the crew had was hard tack or ship's biscuit and the rum or liquor they had brought from Spain.

During this time several steamers – two or three stackers – passed in the distance, but did not see the labouring schooner. On December 21, the crew, knowing the *Harold* was going down, kept distress flags and signals going day and night.

That night the helmsman saw two masthead lights in the distance. Others looked out into the night, but saw nothing. Then, as *Harold* rose on the crest of another tremendous wave, they all saw a large steamer heading westward and in their direction. Captain Yetman had the crew prepare distress flares or to get a small signal fire ready. When the steamer got to within a half mile, every temporary light and emergency flare on the schooner was lit and its small foghorn blew continuously.

The steamer slowed, came close and someone asked through the megaphone what they wanted. Yetman replied, "Take us off as the vessel is sinking."

The steamer's spokesman said they would try to help. It came around to the windward and turned on its searchlights. All this time a winter storm raged across the Atlantic, but the steamer's crew were determined and lowered a lifeboat. It immediately broke when seas drove it against the side of the steel vessel. In all four smaller lifeboats were broken in the slings or damaged when they were lowered.

The officers of the ship – which by this time *Harold*'s crew had learned was the German liner *Koeln* – said they would try the largest lifeboat and if that failed, they would wait until daylight or better weather to take the crew off.

The large lifeboat was prepared, the lifesaving crew climbed in, and when *Koeln* rolled on its side, they pushed off. For a moment it looked as if the lifeboat capsized, but its crew righted it and moved toward *Harold*. One of the German sailors aboard the lifeboat was a young seaman, Karl Herget, but that was not really significant to the Newfoundland sailors at that time.

When the lifeboat neared the schooner, Captain Yetman threw a line to the rescuers. One by one each Newfoundland seaman clambered aboard the boat, but it took an agonizing five hours to effect the rescue – a testament to the ferocity of the elements that night.

When they reached the side of *Koeln*, each person, rescued and rescuers, had to climb an eighteen-foot rope ladder.
*Harold* was abandoned at sea and its crew was taken to Baltimore; in time they reached their homes in Newfoundland.

Forty-three years later the story of rescue and near-death
at sea took a curious turn. In the following decades, Germany had been embroiled both World Wars. By August 1945,
the World War II was over, but the country was devastated,
defeated, many cities lay in ruins, its people hungry.

In September 1947 Karl Herget, perhaps believing that
one good turn deserves another, sent a letter to Newfoundland. It was postmarked Frankfurt-main-Sindlingen, Gustavs
Allee, Germany, and addressed to the Harbour Master at Harbour Grace. In time, the letter was delivered to Mr. A. Simmons.

Herget told the reader (Simmons) he was one of the lifeboat crew who risked their lives to save the Harbour Grace
seamen on the *Harold*, nearly forty-three years previously. But
Hergert's letter was more than a reflection of rescue; it was a
cry of distress, just as the Newfoundland tern schooner had
appealed for help in 1904.

Things were desperate in Germany since the war had
ended in August 1945 and for Karl Herget and his family.
According to the St. John's *Evening Telegram* (which printed
sections of the letter), Herget says: ". . . 43 years have passed
since the time of that rescue. I suppose you know about the
present circumstances in our country by newspaper. Hunger
reigns and there are heavy sorrows about how to feed one-
self."

Herget, perhaps then in his sixties, reminded the reader
of the letter that when Captain Langreuter of the *Koeln* called
for volunteers to man the lifeboat, he (Herget) didn't hesitate.
Now, in 1947, Herget continued, he, his wife and family were
in great need and asked that if even one of those men from
*Harold* still lived to help him and his family: "Send some lard,

bacon or oil, tea, milk powder, sugar, coffee and soap. These are things which we know only by name since a long time. I don't beg for delicacies, clothing and so on, only for victuals to keep us alive.

"Send this letter to any survivor of the *Harold*. If that is not possible, deliver it to some reputable organization in New York and confirm the account of the brave deeds of a German lifeboat crew in 1904."

It is not known what success Karl Herget had with his request, but it is highly likely he was sent a care package by one or several of the crew or by some dependable organization in Harbour Grace. The abandonment of *Harold*, the bravery of German sailors and the letter from a despairing rescuer make for a poignant tale of the sea.

# Sources

*Newspapers:*
Bay Robert Guardian
Free Press
Halifax Chronicle-Herald
Halifax Daily Reporter and Times
Halifax Mail
Halifax Morning Herald
Harbour Grace Standard
London Daily Standard
Lunenburg Progress
New York Herald
New York Times
Philadelphia Ledger and Transcript
St. John's Daily News
St. John's Evening Mercury
St. John's Evening Telegram
Saint John Daily Sun
Saint John Telegraph-Journal
Shelburne Gazette
Sydney Post
Twillingate Sun
Western Star

## Publications:

Burgess, Robert F. Sinkings, *Salvages, and Shipwrecks*. New York: American Heritage Press, 1970.

Canadian Coast Guard. *Shipping Casualties off Canada's Atlantic Coast 1896-1980*.

DeSmet, P.J. *Voyage and Wreck on the Humboldt in 1853*. University of St. Louis, 1854.

Saunders, Frank. *Sailing Vessels and Crews of Carbonear, 1981*. St. John's, Newfoundland: Robinson-Blackmore, 1981.

## Archives and Museums:

Public Archives of Nova Scotia, Halifax, Nova Scotia

Beaton Institute, Sydney, Nova Scotia

North Sydney Museum, North Sydney, Nova Scotia

Statistics from Captain Hubert Hall, Yarmouth, Nova Scotia

A.C. Hunter Library and Memorial University Archives, St. John's, Newfoundland

Shelburne County Museum, Shelburne, Nova Scotia

Southern Newfoundland Seamen's Museum, Grand Bank, Newfoundland

Fisheries Museum of the Atlantic, Lunenburg, Nova Scotia

United States National Archives, Washington D.C.